HEROES
OF MY TIME

HEROES
OF MY TIME

Harrison E. Salisbury

WALKER AND COMPANY
New York

First published in the United States of America in 1993
by Walker Publishing Company, Inc.

Published simultaneously in Canada by Thomas Allen & Son
Canada, Limited, Markham, Ontario

Library of Congress Cataloging-in-Publication Data
Salisbury, Harrison Evans, 1908–
Heroes of my time / Harrison E. Salisbury.
p. cm.
"Published simultaneously in Canada by Thomas Allen & Son Canada,
Limited, Markham, Ontario"—T.p. verso.
ISBN 0-8027-1217-7
1. Biography—20th century. 2. Heroes—Biography. 3. Heroines—
Biography. 4. Intellectuals—Biography. I. Title.
CT120.S25 1993
920'.009'04—dc20
[B] 92-43524
CIP

Designed by Ellen Levine

Printed in the United States of America

2 4 6 8 10 9 7 5 3 1

CONTENTS

CONTENTS

PREFACE
On Heroes

WE DO NOT LIVE in the age of heroes. This is not the era of Jefferson, Lincoln, or Commodore Perry. Nor even of Charles Lindbergh. The politicians of our day seldom remind us of Franklin D. or Eleanor Roosevelt. Athletes signing five- and ten-million-dollar contracts do not resonate as did Babe Ruth. Joe Louis towers over today's men of the ring.

I am not much of a hero worshiper. Too many years as a reporter have made me a skeptic. Perhaps this is why I seem drawn more to antiheroes than to those who win the applause of the multitude.

To me, the ultimate hero is that lone man whom we saw at Tiananmen walking out into the middle of Chang-an Avenue, waving his hand and halting the column of tanks, then walking on and disappearing into the crowd before startled soldiers or men in plainclothes could halt him, leaving behind no name, no trace, only that quick glimpse that told the world one brave man did not fear to stand against the armor and the guns.

I do not expect to see his like again.

I harbor deep distrust of obvious heroes. I have seen too many raised to pedestals only to expose their feet of clay. I have not found many statesmen, national leaders, or colleagues who do not have their weak points. That is natural. I expect people to be human, and if they display nothing but virtues my instinct warns that something must be wrong.

In this collection I have passed over the most renowned figures of our times—Winston Churchill, the Roosevelts, Charles de Gaulle, Martin Luther King, John F. Kennedy, Joseph Stalin, Mao Zedong, Mohandas Gandhi. Some of them I knew, some I did not. With contrariness born of my Minnesota heritage, I rejected them. I almost made an exception for Roosevelt, the universal hero of the Depression Days and of World War II. But I finally passed him by, feeling I could add little to his image except the personal thrill he gave to me and my generation in those first one hundred days when he lifted us all out of despond.

By no means do all of my heroes bear names that guarantee instant recognition. These are men and women whose bravery burns in my mind and always will. They have stood alone and fearless in the face of danger and despair. We seldom see this quality in an age of packaged puffery, sound bites, and greed. My heroes blaze in the heavens like lightning on a dark summer evening.

Many of my heroes are flawed. Some are heroes manqué, but despite their blemishes (and these can be grave, as in the case of Zhou Enlai and Nikita Khrushchev), they have inspired me by their conduct in times of great peril. If it seems that I have included a disproportionate number of writers, I have no apology. I believe in writers as a force for change in the world. They make the rulers live up to their promises.

They expose evil, corruption, and crimes, and they give us hope. It is no accident that a dictator's first act is to suppress the press and the poets.

I know a bit about this. I have sometimes found myself the only one in a crowd to cry that the emperor is wearing no clothes. I have been criticized for what I have written by the leaders of quite a few countries, including my own. I see nothing wrong in that. If a writer receives only praise, surely he is not writing the whole truth. The truth is an uncomfortable thing, and no one is more alarmed by it than a president, a premier, a publicist, or a politician. If a writer lacks the courage to go against the grain, he is in the wrong profession. He should take up bookkeeping.

The men and women included within these pages have given me inspiration not only by their courage, a quality all of them share in remarkably diverse forms, but by their faith. They never give up. They undertake tasks no one else would imagine or, if they did, would consider impossible. And they accomplish these tasks by determination, stubbornness, and imagination. These are people who never consider that failure is possible. Often that is why they succeed.

I do not recommend them as role models. But there are many of their qualities that I would like to possess. Often enough they are not pleasant persons in the ordinary sense. They are too restless, too impatient, too obsessed with their goals. They may not have much small talk or much time for those who are not in some manner connected with their ends.

But that is not always true. Some come from that sunny breed who, no matter how possessed by their own aims, are always ready to lend a helping hand, to exchange a cheery word with the weary, the grief-stricken, or those who have lost hope. In a word, they are as mixed a lot as you will find in the human race.

Let me say that the names within the covers of this

volume are my personal choices. No one, I hope, would select the same men and women; there is nothing I abhor more than conformity. Each of them has something to offer each of us— the rarest of qualities in today's cardboard world—personal bravery.

I have included only heroes whom I have known personally or whom I have learned to know well at second remove. This limits me somewhat geographically to areas where I have spent most of my years—the United States, Russia, and China.

HEROES
OF MY TIME

1

Brigid Temple Keogh

THE FIRST GLIMPSE I HAD of Brigid Temple Keogh came on a hot May day in dusty northern Shaanxi. She was a small, almost tiny woman of seventy-eight with thick glasses, and she was already talking before we shook hands. Her tongue did not stop for the next five hours. "You can see I'm an Emmet," she said. That I could, indeed.

What Brigid Keogh was saying was that she was of the tribe of Robert Emmet, the Irish patriot, hanged by the English, September 20, 1803, a tribe numerous and seldom silent.

Brigid and I had a shirttail relationship. I am not, alas, an Emmet and the shirttail existed more in fancy than in fact, but, as she said, God himself would have been hard put to follow the permutations of the Emmets and, perhaps, he would not have thought it worth the effort. Of her being a genuine Emmet, however, there was no doubt.

Brigid Emmet had come to the distant and parched hills

of Shaanxi because this was where Yanan University, a bro-
ken-down Chinese institution, lost in the loess lands at the
end of the world, was located. If there was another university
in all China so poor, so lacking in facilities for teaching, I
could not imagine it. Its very poverty, in a quite direct way,
was why Brigid was here.

I knew a bit about Brigid Keogh before I met her. Out of
the blue she had written me, thinking that I might help her a
bit in making a vision she had about Yanan University come
true. In the five hours of talk that May afternoon I learned a
good deal more.

To her students (although she did not tell me this), Brigid
Keogh was known as *Jui Lao Tai Tai*, "stubborn old lady." She
was that all right. Once she set her mind on a goal, she did
not stop working, thinking, planning, and plotting until she
achieved her end. She was stubborn but only about things
that mattered.

Brigid was not one of those elderly teachers who came to
China after forty years in a Midwestern high school to round
out a career by teaching in an exotic setting. She had spent a
life in distant, unlikely places—Japan, Taiwan, Hong Kong,
Kenya, Indonesia, and Nicaragua. She had been teaching in
Asia for many years when she formed the determination to
come to China. This was in the 1960s when the chances of an
American coming to Beijing were nil. Richard Nixon and
Henry Kissinger had not yet met with Premier Zhou Enlai
and Mao Zedong and together unlocked the gates to China.
There were no diplomatic relations. The Vietnam War was
still under way. Brigid Keogh had decided to teach in China
(on the instructions of her superior), but how to do it? She
decided that Hong Kong was the place to start. What contact
there was between China and the West passed through Hong
Kong. Once there, she found that no official Chinese would
talk to an American. Brigid Keogh did not take that barrier as

2

insurmountable. She discovered one man in Hong Kong who spoke both to westerners and to Communist Chinese. This was Lee Tsung-Ying, editor of the magazine *Eastern Horizon*, a blend of travelog and party propaganda. Lee had a close relationship with the official Chinese News Agency correspondent in Hong Kong, Xu Jiadung, who was, in fact, the unofficial Chinese ambassador to Hong Kong. If anyone could get Brigid Keogh into China, it was Xu.

She managed to meet Lee for lunch and told him her story—she had taught all over Asia. Now she wanted to come to China, both to learn about China and its revolution and to help China in its march toward bringing education and literacy to its vast population.

Brigid Keogh possessed a gift of eloquence as well as persistence. She needed both if she was going to convince Lee of the wisdom of helping her fulfill her ambitions. The Cultural Revolution was past its worst days but was far from over. China was not permitting foreigners to come in. The revolution had generated xenophobia, and Chinese officials did not want to create grounds for incidents.

Even though Brigid Keogh knew these difficulties, she pressed her case and came away believing that Lee "was slightly sympathetic." There ensued a wait. What might happen next she had no idea. Finally Lee invited her to lunch. She had the impression that he would not be alone, and when she arrived at the restaurant she found that Xu was there as well.

The usual Chinese pleasantries were exchanged and then Xu began an inquisition. He was interested in this elderly American and not at all certain of what she might represent, who she might be, and what she actually was up to. She did not seem to fit any pattern he was familiar with.

He began by asking about her personal life. Who was her father? The question embarrassed Jui Lao Tai Tai. She didn't

3

really want to talk about her father because she was afraid
that it would destroy the image she had created of a somewhat
eccentric elderly woman with a special desire to see and help
Red China. She came from a rather important and certainly
well-to-do, if not rich (in the minds of the Chinese), family
from New Rochelle, New York. She didn't think that would
sit well with these proletarian egalitarians, and she wanted to
emphasize her strong desire to help, to contribute through
her teaching to the building of the New China and in the
process learn more about their great experiment. Her background really was very Capitalist and official. Her father had
been an ambassador, and Theodore Roosevelt had appointed
him a judge on the New York Supreme Court. Brigid was sure
that this would make a bad impression and kill her chances of
getting into the Red Republic.

So she fended off the question.

"My father was sixty years old when I was born," she
said. "What difference does it make about him?"

Xu laughed.

"I was the tenth of his ten children," she added, not
bothering to mention the older stepbrothers.

What conclusions Xu drew from that litany he did not
indicate. But translated into Chinese terms, a ten-child family
sounded more like a poor peasant's family than an upper-class
eastern establishment one.

"And what do your brothers do?" Xu inquired.

"Absolutely nothing," Brigid snapped. This was not
precisely true. One of her brothers had accompanied Admiral
Robert Peary to the North Pole. Another had set a record for
a single-manned sailboat crossing of the Atlantic. But Brigid
did not think it necessary to mention these details. She
thought they would only confuse the picture. What they
really proved was that no real Emmet was lacking in derring-
do. How this quality might play in Beijing Brigid could not

fathom. Fortunately, Xu did not seem to feel it was necessary to follow up.

The rest of the conversation went smoothly, and—after a considerable delay—Brigid got the offer of a contract to teach at Beijing University, the number one university of China, established on the base of the old American-sponsored Yenching University. Not until Mao was dead and Deng Xiaoping had taken over did Brigid get her appointment. She was a hit with the students. Her classes were known as the "wonderful '77s," the first class to enter by college examination since exams had been abolished by the Cultural Revolution. She taught English, but she didn't act like her Chinese colleagues. She talked to the students about almost every topic that came into her lively mind. She encouraged the students to argue with her (unthinkable for the solemn Chinese scholars). Brigid delighted her students, and they delighted her. When her first year contract was up, a new contract was signed. All went well in the second year except that she had become the most popular teacher in the university. Students thronged to her classes, and they began to acquire a lively style and an inquiring turn of mind which, in retrospect, Brigid had to admit, was not likely to please the rigid authorities who traditionally viewed Beida, as the university was called, as a potent source of unrest and dangerous thought.

Brigid was not the lone American at Beida. Technically Robert Winter was still carried on the rolls. Winter, in his early nineties, had for years conducted a class in Shakespeare. His lectures were famous. Now he was working on a Chinese-American dictionary and lived on the shores of the university lake, where he swam almost every day until he was ninety. He had become a recluse after being treated harshly by the Red Guards during the Cultural Revolution.

Robert Winter was a relic of the golden Beijing of the 1920s. In those years the city was a pleasant refuge for eccentrics, and Winter had come there in the mid-1920s with his homosexual lover. They moved freely in the Bohemian society of the old city and delighted in its intricate culture. But Robert Winter was living out his years in loneliness, and Brigid befriended him. They had long talks about China and the vanished Beida of his youth, Beijing in the days before the Japanese invasion and the People's Republic.

When Brigid's second year was up, she was not offered a contract for a third year. Robert Winter was not surprised.

"I had been too outspoken," she confessed. "I realized this later. Of course the students loved it. But I went too far. The administration couldn't stand it."

The students complained about her being let go. They wanted to send petitions to the administration. Brigid realized that any effort to continue at Beida was useless. But she did not give up. Emmets don't. If she could not teach at Beida, she would find another university in China.

She went to Hong Kong and sent applications to a score of universities. No replies came. Brigid Keogh is not one to let time hang heavy on her hands. She went off to Nicaragua. Hardly had she gotten there than she received an offer from Hangzhou University. She cabled her acceptance and flew to Japan. There Hangzhou cabled her: So sorry. Complications. Couldn't put her on the staff after all. Brigid decided to tough it out. She advised Hangzhou she was coming on, giving them the flight number and arrival time. This drew a rude response. Hangzhou said: Miss Keogh we have told you that we have no place open for you. We can not receive you.

Brigid gave up. Chinese bureaucracy had defeated her. She took a post in Indonesia. There she got a new cable. It was from Yanan University. They had an opening and offered her a contract. Brigid took no chances. She cabled her acceptance, advised Yanan of her intention to come immediately, and took off before anyone could tell her not to come. Six months before her teaching assignment was due to begin, she turned up in Yanan. The out-of-the-way university—too out-of-the-way to have been warned not to take Brigid Keogh—was impressed by the energetic, strong-willed woman who was so eager to teach at this woebegone spot.

Yanan was a dusty answer to Brigid Keogh's dream of China. It really was the end of the road—no shade trees, no grass, no shrubs, about 1,000 students, a staff of 1,000, and 4,000 family members and dependents. Most of the faculty was there because it was their "iron rice bowl," as the Chinese say, a permanent ticket against starvation. The quarters were grim caves carved out of the loess hills. These were, Brigid knew from reading Edgar Snow's *Red Star Over China*, identical with the caves Mao Zedong and his Red Army commanders had occupied when they came to this forlorn part of China seeking refuge in 1935–36 after the perils of their 6,500-mile march to escape from Chiang Kaishek, settling down there and working out the strategy and tactics that fifteen years later put them in power in China.

Yanan University had been founded in those exciting times. In the decade that Mao and his men spent there they created a series of "universities" and "colleges" specializing in drama and the arts, revolutionary tactics, military skills, engineering, medicine—there were ten at their peak. Not real universities, of course, but cave classes where anyone with expertise was co-opted to lecture to the "cadres," that is, to party members and to Mao's semiliterate commanders who had yet to master the 20,000 Chinese ideographs needed to read a book.

When Mao and his men won the civil war against Chiang Kaishek, the "universities" were packed up and moved to Beijing, where they became the nucleus of today's People's University. Some remnants remained behind and were fashioned into Yanan University, a no-frills normal school to train secondary school teachers for illiterate peasant youth in the north of Shaanxi.

Most classes met in caves or slightly improved caves with facades of brick and mortar and rooms dug out of the loess cliff. They were dirty. The winds blew forever and dust filled your ears, made teeth gritty and hair stiff. There was little water, the river Yan was most of the year a trickle through rocks and boulders. The shops offered remnants and flawed goods too poor to be sold anywhere else, sleazy shoes, ram- shackle stoves, broken shovels, dull axes, rice and beans in bulk and on ration (cotton goods on ration, too). It was precisely to the taste of Brigid Keogh. Here her work would have maximum impact. She could teach and train teachers who were so badly needed to spread reading and writing to people for whom a drop of knowledge was as precious as a diamond.

She was glad she had arrived early. It gave her a head start on getting acquainted.

First there was a struggle over where she would live. The town had built a new, shoddy, and uncomfortable hotel, and the school proposed that she live there. She refused. She would live in the semicave quarters with the rest of the staff. Brigid won and got a bright young Chinese woman to keep her company and help with the chores. Her students, despite their poor preparation, responded swiftly to her enthusiasm. Soon she was taking them for climbs up the hills for picnics on holidays, even though her sight was so faulty she hardly knew where she was placing her feet on the rocky slopes. There were neither real classrooms nor books, no texts in English, none of the apparatus of modern language instruction.

Brigid set about to remedy that. Every post that managed to get through to the hills brought her packages of books and teaching materials. She put them all out for her students to read (not like the Chinese instructors who kept their few books under lock and key). There was a constant queue at her door, students seeking books, and also, begging for the foreign postage stamps on the packets.

There was, of course, no proper place for language studies. Brigid determined to remedy this with her own resources and energy. She had some well-to-do friends and appealed to them. She wanted to raise $150,000, get the university to match it, and build and equip a modern language center. The Chinese were delighted with her proposal. Of course they would come forward with the matching funds. Then the trouble began. It became obvious that every bureaucrat had a different idea about the money. Each wanted it for his or her pet project. The language center was quickly forgotten.

Brigid stood fast. No language center, no money. She saw her project as more than a simple academic improvement. To her, it was the first act in fulfillment of her dream. She saw the center as a step toward creating an education jewel that would sparkle in the diadem of the new China, which the revolutionary peasants had seen as their goal. This was only the first step she envisioned. Beyond that, she hoped to inspire the people to recreate the little town of Yanan as a shrine worthy of the dreams it had begotten.

Her university would be adorned with ivy like the buildings of her adored Cambridge. The Yanan streets would become again the simple pathways trod by revolutionary feet. The caves would be rescued from wind, weather, and oblivion. Once again people would know where Mao's captains and generals—Liu Shaoqi, Zhu De, Peng Dehuai, Zhou Enlai— had lived for ten years. The caves would be cared for, their history taught, their fame recaptured from dimming memories. Visitors would be shown where Mao sat night after night telling the story of his life to Edgar Snow, the cave where the

American revolutionaries Anna Louise Strong and Agnes Smedley lived (tidied up and identified), the lecture hall where Mao gave his "Yanan Talks," and Yanan would become the Valley Forge of China.

She did not underestimate the difficulties. Local commissars had no mind for history or tradition. Townsfolk associated the legends with the teenage Red Guard hordes who descended on Yanan during the Cultural Revolution like devastating ants, a memory they wanted to forget. Now the town was drowned in smoke and smog. You could not see the Yanan pagoda from a quarter mile away. Small ugly factories cluttered the landscape. The roads were a tangle of trucks and carts. More attention was given a cheap cigarette factory that disfigured the approaches than to Yanan University itself.

It happened that I shared Brigid's feeling for Yanan and was shocked at what was happening to the cradle of the revolution. This was a page from China's history whatever you felt about Mao and his Communists.

I was seeing the vice governor of Shaanxi for dinner the next evening, so I had a tactful word with him. I told him of Brigid's plans and the money she had raised. I suggested that she must have encountered some small bureaucratic snag which he could easily overcome. A word from my host would set things straight. And I suggested that success for Brigid's plans could open the way to many more good things. It would be the first step toward an American bridge and creation of a Chinese Williamsburg, if you will.

Apparently, the arguments worked. The bureaucratic barriers fell away, and Brigid's project moved forward.

Twice Brigid had been named the outstanding teacher of Yanan University. Now she was named the number one foreign teacher of the province and invited to Beijing, where she was received by Premier Li Peng on October 1, China's National Day, at the Great Hall of the People. The province made a videotape about her for distribution throughout the region.

Of course there were hurdles yet to be overcome, but one day I received a stiff white cardboard invitation to ceremonies for the dedication of a new language learning center at Yanan. Brigid had won out, and she wrote an article for the occasion:

"I am part of Yanan. I feel loved and trusted. I have shared the frustrations of longing for self-improvement, the hopes of youth trying to graduate from the countryside. I have drunk beer with them, played bridge with them, joked with them, argued with them, dreamed with them. I have been frustrated by them, amazed by them, enraged by them, but always helped and uplifted by them. I feel part of the great struggling Chinese countryside."

What Brigid had done did not go to her head. She was an Emmet, and there was always another river to cross. She was already planning the next steps. True, she was relinquishing her teaching post. Her eyes had become so bad she could no longer get about the stony trails and dusty paths. She would have to retire to Japan. But she was not giving up stewardship of the university. Already she was sending some of her students to the United States on scholarships. She was using her network to build for Yanan's future. So long as she lived she would go back to Yanan again and again to help push it along. She could not bear to think of Yanan sinking back into despond. A railroad had finally come, ruthlessly smashing Liu Ling, the Willow Grove farming cooperative that Mao and his comrades had helped set up as a model for what they planned for China. Never mind. That was progress that could not be thwarted. What she wanted was to protect, encourage, and enhance more soaring dreams. I had no doubt that Brigid—with the aid of her fellow sisters of the Roman Catholic Order of the Sacred Heart from which she had

11

finally retired as mother superior, in charge at Vatican direction of the China program—would prevail against whatever temporal forces the bureaucrats might array against her.

What, I thought, would Mao have thought had he known that an Emmet nun was leading the fight to keep alive the Yanan tradition? And what, too, would the pope say of this twentieth-century sister working single-handedly in her own way, as had the Jesuits of the fifteenth century, to bring China into God's kingdom?

2

Robert F. Kennedy

ONE EVENING IN OCTOBER, 1956, I found myself sitting on the rails of the B & O track in central Ohio, the dusk gently settling over the flecking yellow paint of the depot and a soft vesper breeze stirring the air.

Sitting beside me on the rail, his legs sprawled out and heels dug into the sand, plucking grass from between the rails, chewing the stiff stems, then spitting them out, was a lean young man, his almost chestnut hair tousled by the wind, slowly asking questions. He was Bobby Kennedy, and it was the first time he and I had exchanged more than a casual hello.

I did not like Bobby Kennedy. I didn't like his manner, his style, or his questions. He was hard eyed, hard faced, hard minded, and thin lipped. He seemed casual, but I did not think he wasted a gesture and I was certain his quick eyes did not miss a thing nor his ears a word.

I was covering the presidential campaign of Adlai Stevenson that autumn. Bobby had joined the party to represent his brother. I liked Adlai Stevenson a lot, but I did not think he was going to defeat President Eisenhower. Bobby shared my opinion and took no pains to conceal it.

Stevenson had a weakness which Bobby's presence was designed to ameliorate. Adlai was a divorcé, and in 1956 this was a major negative. His nomination had been opposed by many big city Catholic bosses. Bobby was supposed to be a bridge to the Catholic bosses and Catholic voters, but, in fact, as I knew, Bobby had come along without the slightest intention of helping Stevenson. The Kennedys could hardly wait for Stevenson to lose to begin their campaign for Jack in 1958.

Still, I thought Bobby might at least go through the motions. He could have appeared at Stevenson's side in the Catholic towns and made a few calls to the Catholic bosses. Not Bobby. Not once did he lift a finger. But Bobby was not inattentive. His bright eyes caught every detail of the campaign. It was, I must admit, rather sloppy. We didn't get to meetings on time. The speeches were never ready. The candidate was scheduled into windy open-air plazas with microphones that didn't work. We arrived too early or too late. The baggage got lost. Sometimes the candidate got lost. Sometimes the press cavalcade went one way, Stevenson another. We never caught up with our laundry.

Bobby took it all in. He would be running a campaign for his brother in 1960. The Stevenson campaign was a rehearsal, a learning experience. Stevenson's mistakes would not be duplicated. This did not endear Bobby to me. He was a hard-nerved political operator, I thought, a typical Kennedy. And I did not have much love for the tribe.

I had known about Old Joe, the father, long before he became a national figure. I had been a newspaperman in Chicago in the late Prohibition years. Old Joe had made his stake in 1929, smart as a tiger, piling it up when everyone was losing his shirt. Smart, there was no other word for him. And he worked the shady side of the street. Deals. Other people's misfortunes were Old Joe's chances. That was how he acquired the Chicago Merchandise Mart, which Chicago proclaimed as the world's biggest building. It had been finished in 1930 and had been empty ever since. Joe picked it up at a disaster price. When I got acquainted with it in 1932, the mart was still vacant except for a block-long bar in what we fondly thought was the largest speakeasy in the world. The bar business was wonderful. Drinks were a bit expensive, but the free lunch was magnificent. I never knew whether Old Joe owned the bar, but we thought he did and it made someone a lot of money. To me, the speakeasy symbolized Kennedy—an operator on the make. That and the rumors of Old Joe and Scotch whiskey during Prohibition's rum-running days and in a Kennedy monopoly of good brands after Prohibition.

Old Joe had been a financial backer of FDR, and he got a fine reward—chairmanship of the new Securities and Exchange Commission. Roosevelt thought he was putting a superfox to watch the smaller foxes. I doubted that the superfox lost many chances for profit. Then came the ambassadorship to England, Old Joe's antagonism to the war, his anti-Semitic bent, his fondness for the Axis. I thought it passed all bounds of excusable Irish anti-Englandism. But I had to concede that the Kennedys paid their dues with the death of young Joe, flying a Spitfire for England.

I set young Bobby against that background, a hard youngster, as hard as his father, harder than his brother Jack, and a friend, to boot, of Senator Joseph McCarthy. This was the young man who sat beside me on the B & O tracks, and I was not a little surprised that he should be there.

But Bobby wanted to talk to me because I knew something he wanted: information about Soviet Central Asia. I

had been there more than once, and in his direct, prosecuto-
rial way, Bobby proceeded to cross-examine me. He and
Justice William Douglas were planning a trek to Turkmania,
going in, I gathered, from Afghanistan, and he wanted to
know what conditions they were likely to find when they got
to Tashkent, Alma Ata, and Samarkand. He did not make
clear the objective of the expedition. They were going, I
concluded, because Soviet Asia was there, like the Himalayas.
It was a difficult place to get into and difficult once you got
there. That seemed to sum it up. We had a long talk. I had
filed my story for the night. We had nothing to do until
Stevenson came back from whatever god-awful place had been
selected for his meeting.

The conversation deepened my negative image of Bobby.
He was shrewd, smart, totally Kennedy-directed, totally im-
personal. I didn't like him, and something about his Asian
trip gave me the feeling I wasn't going to like that either.
When Bobby and Justice Douglas wrote their inevitable book,
I thought it was pretentious and superficial, drawing headline
conclusions from minimum evidence. I had no contact with
Bobby for a long time after my review appeared in the *New
York Times*.

I DON'T THINK I saw Bobby again until West Virginia in
1960. Jack was running for the Democratic nomination against
Hubert Humphrey. Ted Sorenson, Arthur Schlesinger,
Kenny O'Donnell, and the rest were busy buying West
Virginia. No one would prove it, but everyone knew that a
vote for Kennedy was worth $5 in 1960 money. The district
leaders had stacks of cash and spread it around. Of course
Kennedy won. I listened to the West Virginia returns with
Averell Harriman. "They just used their money," Averell
said. "They bought it." Certainly it wasn't the first American
election bought and paid for, but I didn't like it. I knew by

now that Jack Kennedy was better than this. He was intelligent, wonderfully witty, had a very smart campaign staff. He could have taken Hubert head-on without the $5 passouts. Jack was ingratiating himself now with the newsmen. They were coming to think he could do no wrong—he was one of them. I didn't buy that. I rode back to New York one night alone with Jack in his plane. He spent an hour cursing the correspondents. They never left him alone. They couldn't write a decent story. They couldn't let his father alone. Awful people. I often thought of that evening when I read the tender, romantic prose about Camelot.

I gave Bobby credit. He didn't pretend to be buddies with the press. He was too busy with practical details, the deals, the winks, the bosses, the money, the dirt (on Nixon or on Jack). Of course I preferred JFK to Nixon, but I was not bowled over. I am afraid I took to calling Jack "a lace curtain Nixon." It was not unfair. Under the skin the politics of the two men did not differ much.

By now Bobby was becoming an éminence grise. I saw little of him, and nothing I saw changed my notion that he was his brother's man, heart, body, and soul. Where his brother was concerned, I did not think he had a scruple. He seemed more and more a character out of Shakespeare in modern dress. In one of the tragedies, a man with belted sword, a short-bladed dagger, and eyes that roved the horizon.

I WAS GLAD when Jack won the election. I now knew that he had the ability to do the job and more. But where Bobby fitted in I had no idea. I was amazed when Jack slipped him into the cabinet as attorney general. Postmaster general was one thing. But attorney general? That young mafioso? What did he know about the law? My second thought was—Jack is going to run the Department of Justice from the White House, and all enemies of the Kennedys better beware.

But I had not thought it out clearly. If Jack put his brother into that slot, there must be danger. Not just a matter of using the law. And of course that was it. The danger was J. Edgar Hoover. I had not known much about J. Edgar at that time. I did not know he was an implacable enemy of the Kennedys. Bobby was there not just to manipulate Justice; he was there to protect Jack and the Kennedys from a clear and present danger.

I began to understand this better when my friends told me about conditions within that great limestone pile of many corridors. Bobby and his close circle of aides never discussed delicate matters in Bobby's office or on the telephone. They went out into the corridors and paced up and down. Or they took a stroll on the Mall. If Bobby and Jack had to talk urgently by phone, they used the Kennedy patois of their childhood. It was, in effect, a presidency besieged by an enemy within.

I BEGAN TO SHIFT ground on Bobby during the civil rights crisis. I knew something about the perils of the Mason-Dixon line. I knew all I needed to know about "fear and hate" in Birmingham. My reports of it had brought down on myself and the *New York Times* libel actions amounting to millions of dollars. It was a dark and bloody ground. I thought Jack was late in moving in. But I did give Bobby and his team all credit for bravery. This was a real battle, and they and the president understood it. I had never doubted their courage. Now they were standing as they needed to stand.

Perhaps, I began to think, Bobby is beginning to grow up. His lip still curled like that of a sulky child; he still gathered his team around him, his feet on his desktop, as though he was laying plans for a raid on the Yalies; but his acts were acts of manhood.

When November 22, 1963, changed the world, Jack

became a martyr and I thought Bobby was doomed to be an acolyte at his brother's shrine. I felt deep sorrow for Bobby. He had been capo to his brother. Now he was head of the clan. He had to grow up very fast.

Bobby ran for the Senate from New York. There was a Kennedy slickness about that race I didn't like. True, there was a slot. But New York? Bobby was Massachusetts. He hadn't learned the Kennedy accent in Riverdale. Every time he opened his mouth he reminded you of that. I believed he would make a good senator. But it should have been from Massachusetts.

I couldn't help wonder whether his brother's death might shroud Bobby for the rest of his life. Could he become a fully healthy person in his own right?

His relationship with Lyndon Johnson was muddy. I knew Lyndon hated and feared Bobby, and Bobby made clear to me one day in a quiet aside that he returned the favor. In some crooked fashion I thought Bobby blamed Lyndon for his brother's death. Certainly not complicity in any plot but possibly for creating the atmosphere that led to Oswald's action.

I could not figure out where Bobby was going. He criticized the Vietnam War (which he had so eagerly supported) and seemed to want to strike at Johnson—but how?

I heard the rumors about Bobby and Marilyn Monroe. I hoped they were true. Marilyn had made a good choice if she had decided to give herself to Bobby, a better one than many. It seemed to me that Marilyn could bring a bright halo into a life that I had begun to sense was slipping into dark chambers of despair. The Kennedy rainbow had been shattered, but Bobby was too good to doom his life to mourning. I thought Marilyn would help to lift Bobby out of it.

I HAD HOPED Bobby might test his strength against LBJ in the 1968 New Hampshire primary. He did not. He let Eugene

McCarthy carry the torch. After McCarthy's stunning showing, Bobby threw down his challenge to LBJ. This, to me,
showed a whisper of Kennedy calculation, but by this time I
thought the country needed Bobby. We needed him to bring
us in out of the Johnson nightmare. Perhaps Kennedy calculation was the price.

Then Johnson pulled out March 31, 1968. I cast my
doubts aside. I liked McCarthy. He was a fellow Minnesotan.
So was Hubert Humphrey. But Bobby could beat Nixon. He
possessed the cold steel. I did not trust my fellow Minneso-
tans to cope with Nixon.

In May I spent a cool overcast Saturday on the Hudson
River on the sloop *Discovery*. I sailed up the river with a
throng of conservationists, environmentalists, and politicians.
It was a stunt to dramatize a campaign to rescue the Hudson.

I had not had a long talk with Bobby since the Stevenson
days. He looked much the same—the wind-blown hair, even
more wind-blown on the open deck, the same serious face,
more mature now, a sense of loss in his hollow cheeks,
crinkled eyes that ranged widely but somehow with more
depth and breadth. The 1956 Bobby had a muscular hard-
ness. Now this had softened, diffused perhaps with a sense of
emotion. His talk was different. He spoke, as always, in the
light Boston accent, but his words were different. More
tentative. More searching. The vocabulary of touch football
was gone. He posed questions to himself. The Bobby of 1956
had all the answers. It was all neatly packaged in his brain.
The Bobby of 1968 knew there were questions to which no
one, not even a Kennedy, had the answers. Then he had been
at mission control. Now he was a seeker in a world that was
no longer finite, no longer built of numbered parts that fitted
neatly together like a child's playhouse. The world was composed not just of solids but of gases and fluids and currents
which could not be seen by man or held in his hand.

The new Bobby was a proud man but a humble one. He was no longer a capo. He was a member of the human race, a man of doubts and uncertainties. This was not the Bobby Old Joe had created in his image. Old Joe had not taught compassion to his sons. Victory was all. No tears for a loser. Defeat was unmentionable. The Kennedys' eyes were always dry. They won. The others lost. They won because they were better—better trained, smarter, worked together, never imagined defeat. They were a band of brothers.

But the Bobby of 1968 was a man of compassion. He could not sorrow over what he could not attain, what he could not control. No longer was he a young god. The death of John F. Kennedy had brought an apotheosis to Robert. He possessed now what he had never possessed—pity. It was not just the death of his brother. It was the fact of death itself. Death had long been a companion to the Kennedys, but they had not looked that way. They had not admitted it into their lives. When young Joe died, his brother John ritualistically stepped into his place, the obligation to be the first Kennedy president assumed. Now Robert had stepped into his brother's place, and the mantle had come over his shoulders. In doing so it had brought to Robert knowledge of mortality and humility. He understood life as he had never understood it before because he understood death. He spoke not as a superachiever, not as a capo, but as a whole man whom tragedy had tested and found true, a man who had fought his way back from the brink.

I knew as I talked with Bobby on the windy boat and saw his eyes rove the grandiose scenery of the early American dream, the magnificent crags of Washington Irving's legends, the great crest of West Point, that Robert Kennedy had become what I never thought he could be: a man. He would be president. He would win the presidency and become our greatest since Abraham Lincoln. He had Lincoln's sadness in his eyes. I listened to his quiet, cool speech and heard the pauses as he searched for the right thoughts to express what he wanted to do.

Gone was the smart aleck. Gone was the political trickster. Gone was the shallow sureness. Robert F. Kennedy had come of age.

We docked in midtown at dusk. I walked off the pier with great emotion. I had been talking with a man who had descended into hell and had climbed his way back.

I could hardly wait until November. I had not the slightest doubt that Robert F. Kennedy would win.

IN THAT YEAR of 1968 I was the editor of the *New York Times* concerned with political coverage. On the evening of June 4, I stayed at my desk at 229 West Forty-third Street until nearly 1:00 A.M. Robert Kennedy was speaking in Los Angeles at the old Ambassador Hotel. I left only after his talk was finished and took a cab to my house on Eighty-fourth Street. Hardly had I arrived than the telephone rang. Robert Kennedy had been shot. I raced back to the *Times* and spent most of the night there. I knew from the first bulletins that only a miracle could save him. I didn't believe in miracles, but I stayed on the desk, grabbing for each new bulletin. Twice the telephone rang. It was Jackie Kennedy calling to ask if there was any more news. Her voice seemed to float over the wire from some distant vale. I did not think she was really conscious. Each time I tried to tell her something comforting. There wasn't anything comforting, but I could not speak the truth. Not long after her second call the bulletin came through. Robert Kennedy was dead.

I had not cried when Jack died. I am not much on crying, but when I got home and awoke my wife, Charlotte, I burst into tears. The last bright hope of America in my day had been snuffed out. That is what I felt at 3:13 A.M. on the morning of June 5. And that is how I feel today.

3

Deng Pufang

THE FIRST TIME I WROTE of Deng Pufang I described him as a big, strong man, quite a lot bigger than I had expected, making two of his father, Deng Xiaoping, who was less than five feet tall. Pufang was bigger in every way—taller, broader, more muscular, with heavy features and a round face. No sign that he was a cripple.

Deng Pufang had plunged from a four-story window during the Cultural Revolution in 1966, breaking his back. That crippled him from the waist down. He did not know how he went out the window. Did he jump? Did he roll out, unconscious? Or was he pushed?

He did not know because he had been beaten to a senseless hulk by sadistic Red Guards, determined to "suicide" him as the "black spawn" of his father, the "Number Two Capitalist Roader" in China.

Young Deng was a brilliant physics senior at Beijing University when it happened. He had, like all students, joined the Red Guards in the frenzy to venerate Chairman Mao. When Deng Xiaoping's name went up in the *dazibao*, the large-character posters, the Red Guards turned on their classmate.

Deng Pufang was beaten mercilessly in an effort to make him confess to the evil deeds of his father. When he remained silent, he was thrust into a small closet, the walls red-stained with the blood of earlier victims.

Here he was kept in blind darkness, no food, no water, until brought out for more torture. He was beaten unconscious, revived with a bucket of water, and dumped to the floor of a stripped-down room. Door fittings and windows had been removed. He remembered being told that the room was radioactive, an old laboratory. If he stayed there an hour, he would die of contamination.

The window space was open and frameless.

That is the only way you can get out, he heard them say, then lost consciousness. The next thing he knew he was lying in the courtyard, four stories down.

The Deng Pufang I met in 1987 bore no mark of these tragedies on his countenance. He sat upright and active, talking freely, no sign of physical disability except that twice within the hour a young man entered, deftly slipped to Pufang's side, and rearranged his legs. Not a word of his physical history did he relate. Meeting him I had the impression of a man in the prime of life (he was forty-eight in 1992), an active, outgoing young executive, talking crisply and competently.

He told of his work with and for China's thirty million disabled. When, at a later meeting I asked about his injuries, he put me off, insisting they were not important.

What was important, he said, was what had happened to China in the Cultural Revolution.

It had been a disaster for the country, for the party, for

24

the whole people. You can say, he exclaimed, that we were all victims, not just one generation but several generations, a hundred million victims of all ages and of all strata of life, some in their teens, some in older generations. The whole structure of the country was weakened. Ideals were destroyed. The confidence of the nation was jeopardized. The economy was driven to the brink. Ethics vanished. It was a time, as a woman put it to me, "when we all became beasts. We were like animals or worse."

Compared with this, he felt that any personal loss was small.

"The damage to the minds has been more serious than the physical damage to bodies," he observed.

More than ten years after the Cultural Revolution the damage, he believed, was still present in the minds of people. But now he felt the country was moving out of the shadows. It might take one hundred years, but China was on the way. He cited his campaign for the handicapped as an example.

Deng Pufang was forty-three when I first met him at the offices of the association he had founded for helping the handicapped. This was only the first step. He was trying to change China's philosophy toward those who suffer disability. Humanitarianism was not strong in China's tradition. In the days of princes and landlords charity consisted of presents and a handout on great holidays—conspicuous spending, as Veblen would have said, not from a sense of noblesse oblige. The responsibility of the more fortunate toward the less fortunate was not part of the Chinese ethic. It was not stressed by Confucius or Buddha and was opposed by the Communist Party. Karl Marx had declared charity nothing but a device by which the rich enslaved the poor. Following Marx, Lenin had refused to aid the starving Volga peasants in the famine of 1893. His heirs in China adopted the same posture. Charity was frowned on or forbidden.

I had gone to the offices of Pufang's association to participate in a ceremonial meeting, and it opened a path to a friendship that gave me deep insight into this man, his hopes for China, and also an understanding of his father and his family.

I respected Pufang's courage and the scope of his determination to change China. His decision to dedicate his life to his country came directly from the Cultural Revolution. Not only had his back been broken, but he was denied any treatment. How long he lay unconscious below the window he did not know. Finally he was hauled to the university hospital and held prisoner there with no medical attention. He could not sit up. His legs and body were paralyzed. He could hardly hold a bowl of rice. The Red Guards expected him to die. He did not.

Finally he was sent to a dirty clinic, again given no medical treatment. He earned a few yuan to pay for his meals by weaving wire wastebaskets lying flat on his back. He credited a young worker named Wang Feng with saving his life. His family was not permitted to help. Deng Xiaoping and his wife were under house arrest, confined from 1969 to an abandoned military school. Frantic appeals to allow doctors to examine their son got no answer.

Pufang spent much time thinking about China and the causes for its lack of a humane tradition. Finally, in 1968, he was transferred to a center for the handicapped north of Beijing for custody, not treatment. Ten cripples crowded into a dark, damp room. One was Wang Luguang, injured in an auto accident. The two resolved that if they survived they would work together.

Pufang was separated from his family for four years. After the death of Lin Biao, Mao's enemy, in 1971, his parents got permission to bring him to their place of exile. Deng and his wife stripped their son's filthy clothes from his body, bathed, massaged, and cared for him as best they could. Medical aid was still banned. Deng heated the water, and he and his wife carried their son into the bathroom for his massage, letting the room fill with steam.

In these times, as Pufang remembered: "I realized that my father was a real man, a true man, not just another politician like other leaders, his mind always fixed on politics. At home my father was a real father. He loved his children and his grandchildren."

It was a difficult time, but it created a bond between father and son. Permission was finally granted to allow Pufang to be examined by a team of Beijing physicians and then to be sent to Toronto (accompanied by Li Peng, who was to become premier) for diagnosis and treatment. The Canadian doctors performed two major operations. This enabled Pufang to sit upright, although he still could not bend. They wanted him to stay for lengthy rehabilitation, but he refused and returned to China determined to devote his energy to establishing in his homeland a modern rehab center. With Wang Luguang, his bedmate at the clinic north of Beijing, he set up in Beijing in 1983 a national association for the disabled.

The government lacked funds, and Pufang was determined not to burden the state. Contributions came from many sources but not enough. Pufang was persuaded by some of his father's old friends to set up a special financial affiliate called Kanghua. The idea was to take about three million yuan in funds from contributions and use them to create an investment company that would engage in business activities. The profits would go to help the needy. It proved an ill-advised venture. Speculators and individuals hoping to win influence with Deng Xiaoping, now in power, flocked in. Soon Kanghua was known as "the hottest ticket in China." Charges rose that Pufang was trading on his father's reputation. Admittedly naive and without business experience,

Deng Pufang took the blame, then cut all ties to Kanghua. "I know nothing of business," he said. "I depended on older and more experienced men." The men, three old cronies of Deng Xiaoping and former government members, knew a lot about business and were en route to turning Kanghua into a multi-billion enterprise when Pufang cut it adrift.

Finance was not Pufang's long suit. He endured violent criticism for the Kanghua episode. In the Tiananmen demonstrations he bore the brunt of student attack. But no one knowing Pufang could doubt he was an innocent victim.

Pufang's thoughts were fixed not on money but on humanitarianism. In part because China's standard of living was so close to subsistence, peasants had no tradition of mercy toward the unfortunate. In the village a cripple, like a leper, was driven out with sticks and left to fend for himself or die in the fields. The same was true of the infirm, the old, and the diseased. The community could not afford to care for those unable to carry their own burden.

Not only cripples were neglected. So were widows. A widow traditionally could find no second husband. If her husband's family turned her out, there was nowhere she could go—except to prostitution. Many female infants were thrown out like trash; they had no economic value. Only able-bodied people were wanted in society.

Pufang met the problem head-on. He set out his ideas after founding the Association for the Disabled. He recalled that in primitive societies prisoners of war were killed. In slave society they became slaves. In feudal society they became laborers personally attached to the warrior who captured them. Only under capitalism, Deng Pufang told his listeners, did the concept of liberté, égalité, and fraternité become established—prisoners became people with the rights of people. This was a contribution of capitalism that never got to

China. At the time of Mao's revolution the country was still feudal.

"This," Pufang proclaimed, "is capitalism's contribution to society—humanism." He conceded that humanism had sometimes been distorted, but under its banner much had been done to improve the condition of man.

It meant, he said, freedom not only to love people but to love cats and dogs. Confucius, he noted, had spoken of loving people more than two thousand years earlier, but only in theoretical terms. It was not given practical application until the capitalist era. This had widespread influence outside China. But China did not share it because capitalism was so primitive there. The country had not taken part in what he called "the spiritual wealth" of western capitalism. In China the influence of feudal ideas still prevailed. Chinese society was more brutal, more inhuman in consequence.

Pufang pointed out that when Chinese children saw a lame person limping down the street, they did not run to help him but chased and harassed him. He recalled talking to a party official about the plight of the disabled. "Why do you want to work with them?" the man asked. The contrast, he indicated, between the attitude of Chinese party bureaucrats toward the crippled and that of American businesspeople was profound.

This reflected, he believed, the lack of Chinese education in and attention to humanist views and practices. The fact was, he insisted, that Communists did many humanitarian things but shunned the concept. The stock attitude had been to criticize without thinking what was involved.

"In fact," he said, "we have been doing some good things both in the international and the domestic community but at the same time we have daubed dirt on our own faces, damaging our reputation and letting others carry the flag of humanitarianism."

Pufang pointed out that Lenin had inveighed against sectarianism and had urged Communists to draw from all human experience. But in China the concepts of feudalism still prevailed. He labeled the Cultural Revolution "religious fanaticism," feudalism, totally alien to socialist concepts.

Humanitarianism, he insisted, lay in the interests of the vast majority of people. He called on the workers in his association not to limit themselves to assisting the needy. They must carry the banner of humanism to the people and use it as a weapon against China's backwardness.

"People who are ready to give their lives for their cause are the pillars of society," he said. "Both in Chinese and world history there have been many people who have this spirit of dedication. If the nuns in capitalist countries can devote their lives to their religion, why can't we Communists and Youth League members do as well as they do?

"The theoretical foundation of Christianity is that human beings are born with original sin. To atone for one's guilt he or she has to do whatever God wants them to do. This is idealism. We Communists are materialists. We devote ourselves to the cause of the liberation of mankind."

But Pufang added, quoting from the Russian playwright A. N. Ostrovosky: "The most valuable thing for a person is his life. It only belongs to a person once. When he is approaching his end he should be able to say: 'I have devoted all my life and all my energy to the most glorious cause in the world; to fighting for the liberation of mankind.' We should also have this kind of spirit."

The cause that Pufang embraced was as wide as China and as deep as its 6,000 years of recorded history. Not an easy one. He led a crusade to bring China into the twentieth century in its legislation and regulations concerning the hand-

icapped. He fought for and won the admission of the physically crippled into universities and other educational
institutions. He began to win access to facilities that enabled
them to be educated (many had even been shut out of grade
and high schools). He got bills approved to give cripples equal
opportunities in jobs for which they were qualified (many had
simply been barred from the civil service). He fought for care
and treatment centers and for medical attention to the crippled. In all of this his father's support was equivocal. Deng
Xiaoping still believed China too poor to afford western
standards of care and treatment of the disabled.

Pufang did not limit his horizon to the disabled in China.
He drew strength from people in other areas who had similar
problems. In 1986 he met Edward M. Kennedy, Jr., son of
Senator Edward Kennedy. Young Kennedy had had a leg
amputated when he developed cancer in the bone marrow.
The two young men found an immediate affinity—not only
in their handicapped status but in the fact that they came, as
they felt, from families of similar political concern. Each felt
he owed a debt to society. It was a relationship that continued
for several years, tailing off only when young Kennedy moved
into the field of environmental law.

Gradually Pufang's words gained strength and force not
simply because he had a famous father but from the power of
his arguments for humanitarian goals, for a caring people, a
people who recognized the great human talents residing in
crippled bodies, the lack of fairness in a country that excluded
from its ranks tens of millions of its own people.

I did not think China would slip back into medieval ways
of treating men and women once Deng and his son passed
from the scene. There were clear signs that Pufang would
leave a better and transformed China behind him as a monument to the fanatics who left him for dead below that four-
story university window.

4

Aleksandr Isayevich Solzhenitsyn

ON A BLUSTERY DAY IN MAY, 1978, rain threatening from morning but holding off until afternoon, Aleksandr Isayevich Solzhenitsyn delivered a commencement address in Harvard Yard.

Solzhenitsyn was sixty years old. He had, as a child, survived the savage civil war in the Don country, endured years of deprivation and sometimes terror, fought and been wounded on the eastern front in World War II, spent years in Stalin's camps and in exile, and survived a fatal diagnosis of cancer. But never in his life had he faced what seemed to him a peril like that on this May afternoon at Harvard.

That this lean, energetic, military-looking man with his strong face, deep-furrowed brow, and ready word would perceive danger from old grads with whiskey-red faces, intellectual dons, and bright, eager, and excessively polite young men seemed extraordinary to me.

I had known Aleksandr Isayevich for years, but we did

not meet personally until this rainy afternoon. He had greeted me with extraordinary warmth and relief. I knew the feeling of danger was real. His wife had said she was relieved that I was there, and his translator had appealed to me to "protect Aleksandr Isayevich."

If this perception of danger in Harvard Yard seems misplaced (which it was), it provides a glimpse into the mind of this towering figure of modern letters. Solzhenitsyn is not Tolstoy, Dostoyevsky, Balzac, or Dickens, but he is the master writer of his times. He returned from the netherworld of the twentieth century and informed us of its terrors in words so stark and simple they burned into our brains, never to leave. He gave us Ivan Denisovich to stand beside Jean Valjean.

Maksim Gorky painted the horror of Russia's lower depths. Emile Zola left indelible images of man's inhumanity in the industrial revolution. They were outsiders. Solzhenitsyn was an insider.

I once heard Solzhenitsyn turn on Arthur Miller with icy fury. Arthur had tried to tell him about the McCarthy period, the blacklisting, the inquisition, the broken lives. Aleksandr Isayevich cut him off: "No one was killed." No, Arthur admitted, no one was killed. "In Russia tens of millions lost their lives," said Solzhenitsyn. The conversation was ended.

Solzhenitsyn was one of those who survived, and he had dedicated his life to reproducing every pain and wound of his fellow inmates. He took a picture of himself huddled against the cold in his padded Gulag jacket with his Zek number— SHCH 232—sewn on his chest. (Zek was shorthand for concentration camp laborer.) That was the signature of his life. Perhaps more than he realized, Gulag had made him a Zek to the end of his days. The Gulag prisoner sees peril in every moment, every person, every word. He survives by vigilance and cunning.

At Harvard Aleksandr Isayevich responded with the reflexes he had learned in eight years in the Gulag and another four in exile. He had learned to keep his head down, to say as little as possible, to map (if possible) escape routes, to ferret out possible peril, always ready for flight.

At Harvard Yard Solzhenitsyn was violating every Zek rule for safe conduct. Of course he had lived in the United States for some years. To be sure, he had established a safe refuge, a home deep in the Vermont countryside. It was far from possible enemies and protected by an electrified fence and TV surveillance monitor. That was a safe house. And there should have been no excessive danger at Harvard, but this was no ordinary appearance. It had been blazoned across the land.

Not only would he be present but he would be speaking his mind in the heart of the camp of the enemy. Solzhenitsyn was telling the world, and particularly the American world, his bluntest opinions. He would denounce America's young, the generation that filled Harvard Yard, for opposition to the Vietnam War (dooming, he asserted, thirty million Asians to Communist genocide and suffering). He would excoriate rock and roll ("intolerable music") and "TV stupor," the "false and dangerous lack of spirituality" in the life of both young and old. He would indict the American intelligentsia, so numerous among his listeners, for "loss of civic courage," for "weakness and cowardice," "lack of manhood," and "unlimited freedom of choice of pleasures."

Solzhenitsyn would trash the Declaration of Independence for evoking the principle of freedom for the "pursuit of happiness." He reviled the welfare state, America's obsession with physical health, material goods, money, and leisure, its failure to accept a reciprocal obligation to defend the common good, and its refusal, as he saw it, to recognize the difference between Good and Evil.

Solzhenitsyn presented a capital indictment of the American way in the simplest, broadest words he could find. His audience, he felt certain, could not fail to understand, and if it understood, arise in wrath against him. He appeared before them as an Old Testament prophet bringing down perdition on their heads.

To Solzhenitsyn, this was an act of the most reckless daring, but he felt the world had reached a crossroads; one path (America's) led to doom and the other (his) to restoration of man's fundamental belief in God and his abandonment of false idols.

Of the falseness of the American idols, he had no sliver of doubt. The wrong turn had been taken, as he said, nearly 600 years ago by the Renaissance and with the centuries had become more and more engrained. Man had taken the fateful step of erecting his own image in place of that of God. By 1978 he had created a civilization based on humanism, not on God's will. Humanism must be torn down from the temple if the world was to be saved.

All this, to a Solzhenitsyn tempered in the frozen snows, the hunger, the desolation of the Gulag, was not rhetoric. It was dogma as powerful as that of Moses in the Temple. It was a cry for the sinners to repent and find God before Hell swallowed them into eternal flames.

I spent the next evening with Solzhenitsyn, congratulating him on his courage and frankness. He could not get over the fact that he had been listened to with respect and interest. In spite of the rain, not more than twenty-five elderly Harvardians slipped away. The rest stayed to the end—a long end. The speech ran an hour and a quarter in rain that was steady if not heavy, and he was interrupted twenty-five times for applause, mostly polite, dutiful clapping but sometimes enthusiastic as when he said that "the human soul longs for things higher, warmer, and purer than those offered by today's mass living habits." And when he extolled the right of people "not to know," as opposed to being suffused with information by press and TV on every aspect of life, political or personal. I had heard a sputter of boos from the far rear when he denounced opponents of Vietnam, but I doubt if his ear caught them.

Listening to Aleksandr Isayevich's powerful delivery and to the inevitably weaker (and not always audible) simultaneous interpretation, it occurred to me that the listeners probably did not realize the fire and brimstone to which they were being subjected. Even if they had heard and comprehended, I could not imagine them storming the ramparts and tearing the speaker limb from limb.

To me, the occasion was perfect Solzhenitsyn, a grand demonstration of his own civic courage, his role as a magisterial *intelligent*, a member of the intelligentsia who was compelled to speak what he perceived to be the truth no matter how unpleasant and personally dangerous.

All of Solzhenitsyn's life was poured into his Harvard speech, but as time went by his message, his purpose, and even what he said became oversimplified in memories. The failure of America to understand him actually reaffirmed Solzhenitsyn's premise that American civilization was not really a serious one.

I thought he had made a grave but understandable mistake in this conclusion. I have spent a quarter century studying this man. I have talked with him by the hour. I understand his beliefs and, I think, his life. I have read much but not all he has written. In late years he has turned out almost mechanically a succession of historical works, some scholarly studies, some slightly fictionalized history. Yet even with all this, I

know there are corners or perhaps whole segments of Solzhenitsyn that remain terra incognita.

Above all else, Aleksandr Isayevich is a Russian patriot.
He is an *intelligent*. He believes in reason in an almost literal
way. He possesses, as many Russians do, a tendency to
narrow definitions. He is not possessed of much of the quality
of mercy. That he lost in his years as a Zek. In fact he is a
living monument to Stalin's horrors, and this must never be
forgotten.

He started as a far different person, a bright, lively
youngster in Rostov-on-Don deep in cossack country. Not
himself a cossack (he has cossack blood), he knows very well
those proud, brave people who guarded the czars' frontiers.
When young (although he does not like to remember it), he
was a patriotic believer in Stalin as were most of his countrymen. He went to war willingly, gladly. His father had been
an artillery captain in World War I, and his death left his
widow the task of bringing up Aleksandr Isayevich. His good
Orthodox grandmother had him baptised, but the boy grew
up a nonbeliever and remained one until middle age. In his
Zek years he came to admire believers very much, especially
non-Orthodox like the Baptists and Evangelicals. They were
more brave, more kind, more selfless. They helped fellow
prisoners. No one else did. Solzhenitsyn praised their courage, but in the end it was to the Orthodox faith that he
adhered after marriage to his second wife, the able and valiant
Natasha, a dedicated Orthodox woman who became his link
to everyday life in his American exile.

As a youngster, Solzhenitsyn possessed hazy literary and
strong dramatic aspirations. He wanted to go on stage. In the
Gulag he swore an oath to himself that if he survived he
would carry with him the words that would destroy the
system. His being had been almost shattered when he was
arrested, a loyal, patriotic, excellent artillery officer serving

37

with valor at the front, for trivial remarks about Stalin in a letter to a schoolboy friend. He had not learned that no remark about Stalin was trivial.

Solzhenitsyn set his Gulag tasks with care: number one, survival; number two, observation and collection of information about the system and its crimes. He crammed much of this into his mind, entrusting his extraordinary memory to retain it. Other facts he jotted down in what he called his "onion seed" handwriting on cigarette tissue. He spent every free moment recording and hiding and preserving his notes. One week out of every four he devoted to reciting and repeating all he had memorized.

Aleksandr Isayevich had been an excellent military officer. To the end of his days he did not lose his military bearing, shoulders straight, head high, eyes alert. He adapted his command style and discipline to his writing tasks, working twelve, fourteen, sixteen hours a day. He took no holidays, spent 365 days a year in work. Every year or two he took off one or two days. For the rest it was work, work, work. No matter how long he lived there would not be enough time for his labors. He wrote no letters, received no visitors, did not travel. All his energy went into the great effort. He organized his household like a military task force. His wife, Natasha, was second in command and in charge of operations. Modern technology was installed by this ex-Gulag inmate. His wife ran the IBM tape machine on which all his works were composed. Her seventy-year-old mother ran the commissary. She learned to drive a car and do the shopping. The Solzhenitsyn boys made up the support force. Until they grew older, they carried messages within the establishment (Solzhenitsyn worked in a building separate from his house, connected by a tunnel). A young Russian-speaking neighbor handled the minimum of telephone calls and communications. The children were educated at home, Solzhenitsyn teaching mathematics and Russian history, priests from a nearby Orthodox monastery (this was one reason for the location at Cavendish) giving instruction in art, music, and religion.

It was a very tight ship. Every effort went into Solzhenitsyn's crusade: to present the record of the Great Evil, the crimes of communism-Stalinism (actually he dated it all back to Lenin), the Gulag and its works.

Solzhenitsyn began to define his mission in Jehovian terms: "Woe to that nation whose literature is interrupted by force. This is the amputation of its memory. The nation can not long remember itself . . . it is deprived of spiritual unity. . . . Silent generations grow old and die without ever talking about themselves, either to each other or to their descendents.

"This is . . . a tragedy for the whole nation, a danger to the whole nation. And in some instances a danger to the whole of mankind when the whole of history ceases to be understood as a result of such a silence."

It was to arouse America and the West to these perils that SHCH 232 went into Harvard Yard against all his instincts— with head high, looking twenty years younger than his age, garbed in green-bronze trousers and a kind of Buster Brown jacket, wide lapels and flatdown collar—and pronounced anathema. It was anathema not just on America, the twentieth century, and the Third Rome (Moscow), but on Rome itself and the schism in the Christian church which in his belief left the Eastern Byzantine and Russian branch as true heir of the Apostolic faith and Rome as renegade deviant.

All this, I came to understand, was evidence of the extremism of Solzhenitsyn's logic, which caused him to perceive medieval Florence as the ultimate Devil's cavern in which the sins of today's world had their source. He was Increase Mather and the spawn of Cambridge's Great Thunderers, the Philipses, the Thoreaus, the Emersons, the Beechers, the

Stowes, the Radicals of Abolition who saw the world as Black and White, Good and Evil, Light and Darkness, Beelzebub against the God of Israel. Never mind that Aleksandr Isayevich had never heard these names and would repudiate them if he had. The spirit was the same, utter and absolute righteousness against utter evil, the belief that there was no truth but their truth.

As Aleksandr Isayevich said: "For the writer intent on truth, life never was, never is (and never will be) easy: his like have suffered every imaginable harassment—defamation, duels, a shattered family life, financial ruin or lifelong unrelieved poverty, the madhouse, the jail. Even those who wanted for nothing like Leo Tolstoy have suffered worse torments in the claws of conscience."

So, he concluded: "Once arrested . . . without hesitation, without inner debate, I entered into the inheritance of every modern Russian writer intent on the truth: I must write simply to ensure that it was not all forgotten; that posterity might some day come to know it."

This was the Solzhenitsyn of the Harvard Yard, and this was the Solzhenitsyn I knew over the years. His goals changed a bit, that is, he shifted his emphasis from photographic recording of the Gulag to an attempt to recapture all of Russia's history of the twentieth century, the period leading up to the Great War of 1914, the war itself, the Revolution, and the years since 1917. These were the years whose record, he believed, had been lost or distorted by the evil hand of communism. He made it his task to gather firsthand accounts of what had happened and to weave a chronicle in a palimpsest of thousands of incidents and portraits. It was a task that would encompass his lifetime and, realistically, many lifetimes.

I do not really know how Solzhenitsyn explained to himself the failure of the American intelligentsia to come forward and fully engage him in debate of his analysis of the decadence that, he believed, they had brought to the country. I think he put that aside and focused on the Russia that he saw emerging from communism, strong, clear-eyed, cleansed by its persecution, able to see itself and the world whole and new, created in God's image, purged of post-Renaissance decadence.

In Vermont he created for himself a sunny corner of Russia in which he lived in a household that in every way replicated the household of a devout middle-class family of the 1860s—a private chapel, children who were diligent, obedient, talented, reciting the classical poetry of Pushkin or Lermontev as "presents" for their parents at Christmas or New Year's (just as Lenin and his brothers did in the Ulanov house at Simbirsk on the Volga in the 1860s), devout believers in the Orthodox faith, imbued with their father's convictions of the heritage and future of the true Russia, totally bilingual, each with his busy role in what was an almost self-contained Russian household, touched only peripherally (but sometimes tragically) by the alien American world. There was nothing restrictive in this life. It was full, busy, satisfying, and within the compound no discordant notes were sounded.

Not that Solzhenitsyn was a bear sleeping through a long hibernation. He knew what was happening in the world, but characteristically got his bulletins in Russian, listening to the Voice of America or Radio Liberty. This was time-saving and more convenient than the many pages of the *New York Times*.

The world of Aleksandr Isayevich had narrow bounds. Like any wayfarer in an alien land, he often generalized from a single episode. His vision of America and Americans was often cruelly distorted. Time did not correct the distortion. It increased, and his vision of his own Russia came not much closer to reality.

How, you might ask, could someone like myself—with a

41

view of America, Russia, and the world so divergent, so much
in conflict with that of Solzhenitsyn—place him in my pantheon? With many of his beliefs I was in broad disagreement.
I perceived many negatives in the United States. I despised
consumerism, the shabbiness of much American thinking,
the limited vision of politicians. Since I spent much time in
Russia, had many vibrant Russian friends, traveled the vast
expanses of Siberia and the Volga, I knew that Aleksandr
Isayevich's image was growing more and more distorted. He
had composed an idealistic conception of his country that
often bent the lines of perspective.

None of this affected my belief in Aleksandr Isayevich as
one of the great figures of his age, a man of courage, possessed
of passionate devotion to his literary art, possessed of match-
less skill and a coherent (if contradictory) philosophy.

I could violently object to much that he said, but I
perceived the world as a better place for his beliefs. He was a
beacon in a shallow life in which writers and politicians
presented themselves more as dumpling dough than as para-
gons. This was manifest in the manner in which Solzhenitsyn
began to fade from the American horizon after the Harvard
speech. No longer was he sought out by the opinion makers.
His name began to vanish from the gossip sheets that pose as
contemporary intellectual reviews. The New York literary
community dropped his name down the memory hole. There
was no rage or revenge. One day he was there. The next he
was gone. Some said this was because Solzhenitsyn was an
anti-Semite. I didn't agree. He just wasn't "one of us." He
had diverted from the main stream.

This was a tragedy for us, not Solzhenitsyn. As events
in Russia began to pile up, as the pace quickened, as communism crumbled in eastern Europe, as the Berlin Wall came
down, as it became apparent that Lenin's experiment was
desiccating, I watched and waited. It was not long before

Solzhenitsyn appeared on the pages of the Moscow (and Saint Petersburg) press. *The First Circle* was published (in its full, uncut form). *Gulag* began to appear. Solzhenitsyn might be a nonperson on the American literary scene. But like mushrooms after rain, he was springing up everywhere in his native land.

But what of the man himself? Would he return to Russia and take his place as the dean of Russian letters? Perhaps and perhaps not. Perhaps he had lived too long in Vermont with his idealized image of his country. He did not rush back. He would go, yes, so Natasha said, of course, he would go. But first there were the preconditions. His words must be published freely in the form he dictated. No cuts, no bowdlerizing. His Russian citizenship must be restored. The government must apologize and lift the penalties against him. Only then would he go—but, actually not exactly then. First there was his work in progress. He must come to a place where he could pause. Then he would return, and a suitable place for the master must be found, a setting for a sage.

As I watched the events in Russia, hurtling downward, ever downward into a repetition of the chaos and tragedy of 1917, I began to wonder. Would the time ever come? When would Aleksandr Isayevich's long wait end? The Russia that was emerging was extraordinarily different from the image before which he had kept a candle burning during the long exile. Would Aleksandr Isayevich ever see the Russia of his dreams?

5

David Halberstam

IT WAS THE FIRST DAY OF MARCH, 1960, and a warm
spring sun was flooding the shopping mart in the center of
Nashville, just before noon, lots of passersby, some curiosity
seekers, a handful of newspeople, and a cluster of police as I
arrived, having hurried directly from the airport.

I was getting my introduction to the lunch counter sit-
ins staged by black students and now spreading like wildfire.
No one on the *New York Times* understood exactly what was
going on. Scrupulously polite, immaculately dressed young
blacks quietly walking up to lunch counters, sitting down on
the stools, and softly asking for a cup of coffee. When the
white waitress refused—as invariably happened—the blacks
sat there. They said nothing, made no protest, just sat until
the police were summoned; they were arrested and dragged
off to jail.

The sit-ins had begun at about 3:00 P.M., February 1,
1960, when four freshmen from the black Agricultural and

Technical College in Greensboro, North Carolina, walked into Woolworths, sat down at the counter, and asked for coffee. Two weeks later the sit-ins reached Nashville. After initial encounters at the Woolworth, Kress, and McClellan counters, they had struck the center-city shopping complex.

The young blacks from Fisk University had been arrested. As the crowd awaited developments, a tall, wiry young man with a shock of black hair, piercing brown eyes behind heavy horn-rimmed glasses, a notebook and pencil in hand, hurried up to my side. "I'm David Halberstam," he said, "of the *Tennessean* and you must be Harrison Salisbury of the *Times*."

We shook hands. Words cascaded from Halberstam's lips. He tried to tell me the whole history of the demonstrations, of the evolving civil rights movement in five minutes. He talked faster than I could make notes. His exuberance overflowed, and he seemed deliriously pleased to be covering a story with such broad and deep implications. His briefing went far beyond the events of the day. He was the first to tell me about Dr. Allan Knight Chalmers of Boston University's Divinity School who had preached to his students, many of them young blacks, the strategy of nonviolent resistance on the Gandhi pattern. And he talked about the legal basis of the shopping center's attempt to close the doors to one group of patrons while keeping them open for others. He thought the legal grounds were shaky, and he was right.

It was easy to see why other *Times* reporters had mentioned Halberstam's name, and I thought that he would soon be on the staff. I was right. David was just short of twenty-six that March 1, 1960, and his career as "The Best and the Brightest" of the young journalists of the 1960s was taking off. He would become the role model of a generation—and more—of American reporters, a symbol of the aggressive, no-holds-barred, heads-up American journalism that produced

45

Vietnam, Watergate, and so many other exposés of the seamy side of American policy and practice. To many correspondents, he *was* Vietnam.

Those who knew Halberstam at Harvard, class of 1955, and who worked with him on the *Harvard Crimson* remember his inexhaustible energy unleashed by what must have been the world's most active adrenal glands.

His energy was so enormous that looking back on it across forty years, his fellow *Crimson* staffers remembered it as awesome. The *Crimson*'s working "day" did not begin until close to midnight. All hands plunged into a frenzy that made the *Crimson* one of the most exciting of newspapers. The staff would be furiously hacking at their Underwoods when David and his brother, Michael, two years older and also a *Crimson* editor, would suddenly grab two office brooms and plunge into a man-killer game of hockey, using a Coke bottle as a puck. They would smash the puck from one side to another, scrambling over desks and chairs, never ceasing, full tilt for a quarter hour, then collapse, sweat-covered, and beat furiously again at their typewriters.

This went on until about 2 A.M. when the exhausted staff put the paper to bed and headed for their dormitories. Not David. He would gather his staunchest friends and make for Chinatown, there to eat a lavish Chinese dinner, getting home just before dawn.

David was a strong man, six feet tall, weighing about 170 pounds at the time. He entered Harvard at seventeen and graduated at twenty-one in 1955. He did not get his full growth until after college. By the time he went to Vietnam in 1962, he was almost six feet three and a muscular 185.

Halberstam's older brother Michael (dead at a robber's hands in 1981) was slightly smaller, two inches shorter, and thirty pounds lighter. Neither brother participated in organized sports at Harvard.

Halberstam was not an outstanding student. His energy went into the *Crimson*. He used to fall asleep in the library. "I was no good in the classical school framework," he recalled.

David shot out of Harvard like a cannonball, as he put it. He loaded some shirts and a couple of suits into his battered 1946 Chevy, tucked in his record player and stock of old 45 rpms, and pointed south. He knew where he was going. He had a job lined up, and then he would head for the *New York Times*.

He made for Jackson, Tennessee, where his mother had been born and where he had cousins. He called ahead about his job at Jackson, Mississippi. It had blown away. Or perhaps had existed only in the mind of a fast-talking editor who wanted to impress a young Harvard man.

It was a blow. David thought of the people at Cambridge to whom he had said farewell with such spirit, heading south into the "dark and bloody" ground of Mississippi. He was not going back to the North. He got hold of a man named George Lemon Sugg of the Mississippi Press Association. Luck was in. Sugg knew of an opening at West Point, Mississippi, a town David had never heard of, the smallest daily in the state. David called the *West Point Daily Times Leader*. Sister Beulah, the editor's mother, answered. David asked if the job was still open. "The Good Lord Jesus has sent you here," said Sister Beulah. David came from a long line of rabbis, but he took the job. It paid $45 a week. He got an extra dollar for covering the Kiwanis Club luncheons.

David was scared, he remembered, as he headed into the deep South. What was he doing in this strangely alien land? He kept singing to himself "You Gotta Have Heart" as he drove into the Mississippi hill country, poor cotton land, lots of black sharecroppers. Only later would it shift to soybeans, beef cattle, and millionaire spreads.

West Point was a town of 8,000 with one industry, a

sausage factory. David rented a spare room in a clapboard-sided house and got to work. It wasn't easy. The editor-publisher was, as David recollected, "not a nice man." In the evenings David batted out articles for the *Reporter* magazine. He had met its editor, Max Ascoli, who said he was looking to fill an editorial position on the magazine. After writing a piece or two, David went to New York to scout the Ascoli job. He was kept waiting five hours in the reception room, and Ascoli greeted him with the words: "Why are you here?" David went back to West Point.

Twenty years after he left Mississippi, David wrote an article for *Esquire* magazine which headlined it: "Starting Out to Be a Famous Reporter." It hadn't been that much fun. But it was experience. David won a few. He even published the words of Tom Tubb, the state Democratic national committee-man, telling his workers to challenge any black who turned up to vote. "I don't want any incidents," he said, "but I don't want them voting." After the story appeared, his editor visited Mr. Tubb and told David, "I think you ought to know that you have one less friend in town today." When David wrote a story about a night meeting of a vigilante group organized to oppose integration, that was too much. The story was not printed, and in two days David was on his way.

David moved to the Nashville *Tennessean* where he would "spend the four happiest years of his life." Much of the time he roomed with Fred Graham, another upwardly mobile reporter, just out of the Marine Corps and headed for law school. The pair lived in half of a lean-to garage, then found a cabin on the Cumberland River with a float from which they swam and fished. They left that for a flat opposite Nashville's Parthenon, next to Vanderbilt University. They liked the place because they had a good view of passing coeds.

David was now expending his energy on the story of the era—civil rights. He had begun to develop the Halberstam style, boundless curiosity, passion, a sense of what was right and wrong. As his Harvard classmate J. Anthony Lukas put it: "At the beginning David was all energy. Now he began to develop reflectiveness. That harnessed to the energy made him a superb reporter."

He had time for the Nashville scene too. He wrote about a character named Good Jelly Jones and also Little Evil of whom it was said there was a worse evil in Nashville but no one could ever find him. He made a lifetime friend of Chet Atkins, the famous guitarist, and wrote up the "Prisonaires," the musical convicts whom Governor Buford Ellington took around the state to sing on public occasions. All the Prisonaires were life-termers. David befriended a Prisonaire who was in for life on a rape charge and got him released. The man promptly committed another rape and was slammed back into prison. He explained to David, "I've just never been able to help myself."

Bill Kovach, one of the great streetwise reporters of his day, got to know David in Tennessee. They were covering the 1959 primary of Estes Kefauver. David was now at the wheel of a red Triumph sports car. He and Kovach rode about west Tennessee together, pooling expenses and charging full rates to their papers.

David had just discovered Gunnar Myrdal and *The American Dilemma*. Kovach bought the Myrdal book and stayed up all night reading so he could talk with Halberstam the next day.

David wrote an exposé of Lynn Bomar, the Tennessee prison superintendent, a man, in Kovach's words, bald as an egg who looked like J. Edgar Hoover without hair. Governor Ellington called a press conference to dispute David's charges and got so angry at David's questions he threw a Bible at him.

David went to the *New York Times* Washington Bureau in 1960, covering the Interior Department about which he knew nothing and cared less. He volunteered for the Congo war, which no button-down collar *Times* man wanted. Now Halberstam was off and running. It was here, as he later recalled, that he "learned to deal with the fear," the inevitable fear of combat. It helped that his reflexes worked like lightning. He could be in the bomb slit before the shell exploded.

At twenty-seven, David thought the Congo was a perfect assignment. It tested his resources, refined his perceptions, seasoned him to physical peril, gave him a chance to learn how to report war, its unpredictability and agony. Soon he was clamoring for Vietnam. He knew that was his story. It had to be. David's Vietnam was not the 'Nam of later days, the big buildup, the armies of correspondents, the "living room war." His was the dark, dreary battlefield the Americans had taken over from the beaten French, the beginning of the escalation, the immolation of the Buddhist monks, the coups. There were not many reporters in the field when David touched down at Tan Son Nhut airport in the fall of 1962, replacing the greatest war correspondent the American press had ever had, Homer Bigart.

It is too much to say that David Halberstam single-handedly turned the American perception of Vietnam around. The errors of judgment, ill-concealed blunders, the absence of a sensible strategic goal, and the mawkish tactics would have done that even if—as the military openly wished—no press coverage had taken place.

But it is true that Halberstam—through his extraordinary work ethic, his insistence on getting to the scene, his ceaseless probing for cause and effect, his willingness to go to any expenditure of personal time and strength to extract a morsel of truth from a seamless pattern of lies—speeded the process. He set a standard. Other reporters followed. He was competitive but not as regards his fellow reporters. There was never a time when he was not prepared to share the details of what he had seen or dug out. And he gave them physical protection when they could have suffered crippling injuries.

On one occasion, Peter Arnett was targeted by Saigon's chief of police. It was the time of the vicious police raids on the Buddhist temples, and they wanted to teach the correspondents a lesson, to intimidate them. As the correspondents stood outside the temples, a swarm of police officers rushed Arnett and hurled him to the ground. The standard tactic was to get a man down, beat him viciously, kicking with jackboots at his kidneys, inflicting serious, sometimes fatal, injuries.

Halberstam saw the officers throw Arnett down. In a flash he hurled himself across the pavement, smashing through the police assailants like a fullback, spreading his legs wide and shouting in a bull's voice: "Get back! Get back!"

The startled police drew back, Halberstam towering over the Vietnamese like a giant. Before they could regroup, the other correspondents rushed in, forming a hollow square. Horst Faus, the great German photographer, swung his heavy camera in circles from its leather strap to create a lethal free zone.

Peter Arnett was saved. Halberstam knew what the police beatings were like. He had endured a rough one once when Horst had slipped him a film clip. David ran for it, but the police tore after, wrestled him to the ground, seized the film, and beat him heavily.

Halberstam's main force was directed against the American military. He was appalled at the corruption, the moral wantonness of the coat of lies in which they encased their failing operation—anything to protect the reputation of the chiefs to whom they reported. To David, this was not malfeasance. It was a betrayal of the country, an absence of patriotism, and a violation of the military code.

The military launched a violent campaign to discredit

the reports of Halberstam and the other correspondents. This reached a climax in 1963 when the correspondents learned the Vietnamese had taken a bad beating at the hands of the Viet Cong. When they tried to get to the field, the South Vietnamese refused to give them transport. They turned to the Americans and got the same dusty answer.

Next day Brigadier General Richard Stilwell, chief of operations, gave a briefing. He started with a tart lecture to the correspondents. They were not to disturb the commander-in-chief, General Paul Harkins, as they had the night before, protesting about lack of transportation. Harkins was a busy man. He was not to be disturbed in his home.

Halberstam listened to the lecture intently, then leaped to his feet, pointing a finger at Stilwell, and declared: "General, we are not your corporals. We will continue to call Ambassador Lodge and General Harkins until you put us on the choppers, and we will call them at any damn hour of the day that we have to because that is our job. We are not going to take your word for anything that happens if there is the remotest chance that we can see it ourselves. We are here for the *Times* and the AP and the UPI and *Time* magazine, and they chose us to be here. If you do not like us, you are free to write to our editors and ask for a new man and maybe they'll send one. Until then we'll keep on doing what we are doing now."

David sat down. There was absolute silence. Stilwell did not reply. David looked over to Major General Bob York who was standing at one side. York winked.

Of course, the military tried to get Halberstam yanked. It did not work. When they went to publisher Arthur (Punch) Sulzberger, who had been a marine in Korea and loved the military, he wouldn't budge. His reply was to cancel a scheduled Halberstam home leave so no one would think the *Times* had blinked.

This was the complete Halberstam. Vietnam won him a Pulitzer, appropriately shared with Malcolm Browne of the AP, soon to join the *Times*. David came back to New York, wrote *The Making of a Quagmire*, the classic work on the American failure in Vietnam, a powerful reportage polemic, then off for more reporting—always in hot spots. He went to Poland and was expelled because he got too close to the bare bones. There was peril in Poland as well as in Vietnam, but Halberstam shook it off. He knew how to cope with it.

Vietnam clung to him. It never really got out of his blood and his mind, finally leading him to his great work, *The Best and the Brightest*, the analysis of how his generation, the brilliant young men of the 1960s and their equally brilliant mentors, could have plunged the nation into the quagmire that David had discovered when he got to Vietnam in 1962. This work established Halberstam as the most luminous critic of the American scene. He followed the trail relentlessly, to explore the role of the great media complexes in *The Powers That Be*, and then turned to the tragic shambles of greed and arrogance that underlay the catastrophe of Detroit and the rise of Japan to dominate what had been an American monopoly.

David Halberstam's exploration of the failed American dream, powered by a relentless mind and ever-renewing physical strength, was transforming him into the conscience of the American heritage.

6

The Three

MANY PEOPLE CALLED them the Three. Some called them the Poets of Street Corners. Whatever they were called, everyone in Moscow at the end of the 1950s knew of Yevgeny Yevtushenko, Andrei Voznesensky, and Bella Akhmadulina.

Russia had never seen anything like them. When they held a poetry reading, thousands gathered. Often the meeting would be shifted to Mayakovsky Square to accommodate the crowds.

Poetry has always been popular in Russia, not the closet art of the United States. But even Pushkin did not excite Russians like these young people, Yevgeny and Andrei born in 1933, and Bella four years later.

When I went back to Moscow in 1959 after five years of exile because of my uninhibited reporting, they were the first persons I wanted to see. Already they were known from Leningrad to Kamchatka. Their talent, their daring, their openness and comradeship drew thousands to their recitals.

In these days Bella and Yevtushenko were husband and wife and Andrei was best friend. The marriage did not endure, but the comradeship did through the thirty turbulent years to follow.

In those years, as I well knew, every kind of pressure was brought upon the Three to conform to whatever was the party line of the moment. Sometimes they had to stay silent for a while, but they never bowed their heads.

No one could have been more beautiful than Bella as she burst onto the Moscow scene at nineteen, dark Tatar eyes, broad Russian face, a fringe of red-tinted bangs which every girl I knew in Russia tried to imitate, a surprisingly strong voice, and a passion for saying what was on her mind whether about affairs of her heart or those of Russia's leaders.

In Yevtushenko there was lodged the spirit of Siberia. He told me he had been born at a switchman's village of the Trans-Siberian railroad called Zima Stantsia, Winter Station, just around the curve from Lake Baikal. His name betrayed his Ukrainian origins, a blond, blond youngster, weedy and thin as a sunflower stalk swaying in the wind as I watched him declaim his verses as though he was firing at the crowd with a machine gun.

Andrei seemed less bold until he began to declaim his poems, the act turning his China-blue eyes into pinpoints of steel, his laid-back platform manner dissolving into a rhythm that sent the words boiling from his mouth. Then I saw the spirit that had carried him through wartime exile as a child in the grim smoke-and-steel of the Urals.

The Three were as different as could be but bound by a passion for truth and Russian reality which the Kremlin could not contain.

I could hardly understand the courage of the Three. I did not know that one night when Yevgeny Yevtushenko was five years old and living at Zima Stantsia, his grandfather came to his bed, offering him a brandy-filled chocolate. He drew a vodka bottle from his cavalry breeches. The boy and the Red Army veteran touched chocolate and vodka bottle and drank a toast: "To the revolution!" That was the last time Yevgeny was to see his grandfather, led away by the police, charged with treason, and shot in 1938. That same year Yevgeny's other grandfather was shot as a "spy" in the pay of Latvia.

Andrei narrowly escaped losing his father in the perilous retreat of the Russians before Hitler's army. He and his mother were sent to Kurgan in the Urals. His father, an engineer, was trying to evacuate factories in the path of the Nazi advance. He managed to see his family only once in those days, a hectic journey to Kurgan to which he was transporting a factory. He arrived at the izba where his son and wife were housed bearing two presents, a packet of bread and sausage and a thin sheaf of reproductions of Goya's etchings of war. Years later Goya's drawings inspired Andrei's great antiwar poem, "I am Goya," once heard never forgotten.

Nothing in my Russian years moved me as did these poets. They became part of my life. I listened to Yevtushenko declaiming revolution from a Moscow stage and then in New York sat with him for five hours in a lower Manhattan coffee shop as he talked and talked and talked of the life of a poet in Russia, of how Pushkin had been befriended by the czar and tricked into a fatal duel with one of Russia's finest swordsmen, a fate which Yevtushenko thought (in modern configuration) somehow might be his own.

I watched from my study window as Voznesensky sat beside the little pond at the foot of Mount Tom in Taconic, Connecticut, staring at the birches and pines and lazily writing in his notebook, and I shared his excitement over the musical he wrote about Admiral Nikolai Rezanov and his forgotten romance with California in the first years of the nineteenth century.

I listened to Bella as she tossed her red bangs and swore "I'm not a hero, I'm not brave" while displaying the kind of courage the world remembers.

Nikita Khrushchev patronized the Three. Then he turned on them. Politics was politics. Poets were poets. And Khrushchev savaged them in 1962 while visiting an exhibition of contemporary art at the Menage Gallery in Moscow. In gutter language, he hinted they were homosexuals who could be put behind bars for ten years. And to Moscow's finest sculptor, Ernst Neizvestny, a man whose shoulders had been deformed by war wounds, he said, "Only death will correct the hunchback." To which Yevtushenko gently interjected, "Surely, Nikita Sergeyevich, we have come a long way from the time when only the grave straightens out the hunchback. Really there are other ways."

Khrushchev shut up, but a grim time for the Three and Russia's poets lay ahead.

I don't want to suggest that the young people were cowed by the cultural dictatorship of Khrushchev and his bureaucrats. As Yevtushenko said, "It goes without saying that the dogmatists used, still use, and will go on using every opportunity they can find to arrest the democratization of our society, but there is no doubt in my mind that dogmatism is doomed."

To a Russian, Yevtushenko said, "the word 'poet' has overtones of the word 'fighter.' Russia's poets were always fighters for the future of their country and for justice. Her poets helped Russia to think. Her poets helped Russia to struggle against her tyrants." Perhaps that was why so many wound up taking their own lives.

Yevtushenko was the most outspoken of the Three. This was his nature. He was what the Russians call "a civic poet," drawing his subjects from the events of the day, never shy about giving his personal advice to Russia's leaders. He took chances. He was the target of the toadies, the influence seekers, who tattled to the ideological bosses about his outrageous viewpoint. This did not shut him up. He gathered an enormous audience. Hundreds of thousands of letters poured in.

As Yevtushenko said: "We have entered a new age. We are searching for truth in the name of communism. We are looking for it in ourselves. Truth is a tender plant, but it has survived a harsh winter and now it will grow.

Yevtushenko was denounced for lack of patriotism. He did not budge even when the government commissioned Yuri Gagarin, the Soviet's first man in outer space, to lead the attack.

Voznesensky's style was more lyric, more in the classic Russian tradition. His god was Boris Pasternak. He moved to Peredelkino, the little village where Pasternak lived, in order to be close to him in Pasternak's final years when he had been reviled by Khrushchev, compelled to reject the Nobel prize, heaped with abuse, and abandoned by the Russian artistic establishment.

Pasternak had discovered Voznesensky in his first days as a poet. Andrei sent Pasternak examples of his work, and it was Pasternak's encouragement that caused him to give up his study of architecture and plunge into poetry. "I was truly his disciple," Andrei recalled. After Pasternak's death Andrei worked for years to get *Doctor Zhivago* published and to preserve the Pasternak house as a museum.

Voznesensky went on to become a friend and admirer of Allen Ginsberg. His writing, he confessed, was still influenced by ancient Russian art and the works of Le Corbusier. It did not astonish his friends that in the early years of Russian liberation from communism he began to work in a kind of

montage of art and verse. Voznesensky was more experimental
and intellectual than Yevtushenko, who wrote in the bold,
declamatory style of Vladimir Mayakovsky, Russia's great
poet both before and during the Revolution, who ended by
taking his own life in the early Bolshevik years.

The horizon of the Three was vastly widened when they
began to come to the United States, often traversing the
continent, giving dozens of readings and recitations, particularly to audiences of young Americans in the colleges of the
1960s.

Bella's verse was more lyrical than that of her compan-
ions, but her backbone was just as stiff against interference
with her creative life. She and Yevtushenko had met while
attending the Gorky Institute of Literature. Yevtushenko fell
in love almost instantly and celebrated their love in a poem
that some puritanistic Russians felt crossed the border of self-
revelation. After their separation she married Yuri Nagibin, a
novelist much older. They spent time at his country house,
managed by Nagibin's mother. Nagibin's divorced first wife
was the cook. Later Bella divorced again and married Boris
Messerer, a theatrical architect of a distinguished theater
family.

Bella came from the solid Moscow middle class, but she
too lost a grandfather to Stalin's police. Although her style
was different, her philosophy was much like that of her fellow
Musketeers. When spiritual life is repressed, she said, people
turn to the poets as their confessors. People are always striving
for something lofty and spiritual, she believed. Like her fellow
poets, she suffered expulsion from the Writers' Union and
suppression of her verses.

Yevtushenko's bolder course led inevitably to fireworks.
The first came over his poem *Babi Yar*, dedicated to the victims
of the Nazi slaughter of Jews at Babi Yar outside Kiev. He
read the poem at the Moscow Polytechnic Institute September

19, 1961. There was dead silence when he finished, then ten minutes of stormy applause. Yevtushenko took the poem to the *Literary Gazette*, the leading popular literary newspaper. The editors read the poem, all asking for copies. But, said Zhenya, I brought it for you to publish. A long night of consultation and deliberation followed, but at about 2:00 A.M., Zhenya watching, the presses began to roll and the new issue with the startlingly frank verses by Yevtushenko came off the presses. It was a milestone in the history of polemical poetry in Russia. Another followed. Yevtushenko wrote a poem warning against the return of Stalinism. Stalin's heirs, he said, were still alive, still planning a comeback. He sent this directly to Khrushchev, and on October 21, 1962, it was published in *Pravda*.

But the curtain was coming down. Swaying with the political winds, Khrushchev cut back his support of the Three. By 1964 he himself was ousted and the era of Leonid Brezhnev ensued.

Andrei Voznesensky was denounced in 1967 as an "agent of the CIA," just as years later Yevtushenko would be denounced as an "agent of the KGB." Voznesensky fulminated about "lies." His trip to New York to appear at Lincoln Center was canceled, and a torrent of filth was dumped on him.

Voznesensky aimed a bit of doggerel at his critics, telling them their words were more appropriate to a Paris pissoir than a literary discussion. He wrote:

> I am suffocating from slander,
> Your badgering, your condemnations
> are yellow, yellow, yellow.

Voznesensky said he was not plotting to "burn down Russia, to serve jazz nor, of course, the CIA!"

"What a distance you are from life!" he retorted to his

critics. "You stink of formaldehyde and incense." He signed off with a tart speech to the Writers' Union board: "It has been said that I must never forget the stern and severe words of Nikita Khrushchev. I shall never forget them. I shall not forget not only those severe words but also the advice Nikita Sergeyevich gave me. He said: 'Work.' For me now the main thing is work, work, work. What my attitude is to my country, to communism and what I myself am, this work will show."

In the long, gray Brezhnev years the Three continued to write, to read poetry, and to travel to America. In fact, some of their critics insisted they had one foot in Gorky Street and the other planted on Broadway. They did, perhaps, write with a bit more care, keeping watch over their shoulders to see what the molasses-style Brezhnev team might have in mind.

Now Stalin is dead, Khrushchev is dead, Brezhnev is dead, the Soviet Union is dead, communism is dead—or is it? But the Three survive. They still join hands. They no longer are the "rising young poets of the 1960s." Zhenya and Andrei are nearly sixty. Bella is fifty-five. Their voices are not crying out the strains of a new generation. They spend a good bit of time in the United States now, often teaching and giving seminars in colleges, all of them but Bella. She visits abroad but not so much. They write but not so much as before. Yevtushenko writes mostly in prose. He is writing a series of memoirs and novels drawn from life. Andrei seems more of a poet, but he is fascinated by the discoveries he is making in his combination of words and graphics. Bella writes as she always has, beautiful, clear lyrics. Now she is more and more compared with the great Russian women poets of the twentieth century, Anna Akhmatova, who lived through the Leningrad seige and spent hours, days, and weeks standing in line to send packages and (she hoped) receive news of her son, a victim of Stalin's prison system (her husband, Lev Gumilev, had been shot by the Bolsheviks), and Marina Tsevtaeva, the tragic poet of revolutionary days who took her own life in want, suffering, and tragedy.

The Three go on, brave as always, fearless, looking to the future, for, as Yevtushenko once wrote:

> Poetry is a kingdom
>   in which the truth rules in every city,
>   Where one is judged both for poverty and riches
>   Where the ruler is whoever becomes its slave.

7

Malcolm X

ON A RAW EVENING IN MARCH, 1963, I shared a taxi
with an old friend up to Lenox Avenue and 116th Street
around the corner from the Theresa Hotel. We were dining
that night with a man who Meyer Handler, my colleague in
the United Press bureau in Moscow in 1944 and later on the
New York Times, thought might become the "black Lenin."

My impressions of that evening are fragmentary. I remember the Muslim restaurant, scrupulously clean, white, a
floor of small, well-worn tiles, a white formica-topped table.
No white customers other than ourselves.

I was not a frequent visitor to Harlem. The last time I
had been in the neighborhood was during Fidel Castro's
United Nations visit in 1960. I had seen Castro at the Theresa
Hotel where he and his mission occupied a floor, bringing
with them their own live chickens to be slaughtered and
served up for dinner. I had seen Castro a day or two before

he spent a couple of hours with the man I was seeing this
night.

I had come to meet the new black Lenin at Handler's
urgent solicitation. Handler had been assigned to examine
new political and economic forces in the black community, a
project which I had launched as national editor of the *New
York Times*.

I respected Handler's judgment. He came from an intellectual background, a graduate of the University of Chicago
in the high tide of the 1920s, and had gone to Paris where he
worked for United Press during the dangerous years leading
up to Hitler, the appeasement of Chamberlain and Daladier,
and the nascent fascism of Pierre Laval.

I was skeptical of Handler's discovery of a black Lenin,
the man rapidly becoming known as Malcolm X, but Handler
was a serious man. He knew the Nazis and he knew the
Communists. He had spent several years in Moscow and then
gone to Tito's Yugoslavia. He had been filled with ironic
delight watching the Yugoslavs pick their way toward a Marxist state by doing everything the opposite of the Russian way.

At the Muslim restaurant that evening, well lighted,
scantily filled, and somewhat austere (signs proclaimed: not
"No Smoking" but "Smoking Forbidden"), I met a handsome,
tall man, self-described as a "very light-skinned Negro,"
somewhat reserved, very polite, very thoughtful. I had met
most of the black leaders of the civil rights movement, but I
had met none like Malcolm X, whose real name, I learned,
was Malcolm Little. I knew from Handler that he was in a
period of change in his thinking. He had come to prominence
as the spokesman for Elijah Muhammad and the movement
known to the public as the Black Muslims but to itself as the
Nation of Islam. I had no idea until he told me why he was
called "Malcolm X." The "X" represented his lost African
name.

I felt that evening that I was not in the presence of a political leader so much as a well-studied teacher who was leading an ignorant and somewhat recalcitrant pupil through first lessons in the reality of a world completely beyond the reckoning of the newfound white middle-class student.

Malcolm X conveyed an attitude of patience, even tolerance, for his pupil, but I had the impression of a surging personality kept in check by an equally powerful will. I did not think this was a man whom I would lightly cross.

There was no hint of ingratiation in Malcolm X. I knew from what I had read that he had no tolerance for whites. The white man, he had preached, was the devil, the root of all evil so far as color was concerned. I quickly found that this fiery view publicly expressed with shattering effect did not resonate in the quiet, thoughtful conversation of that evening.

In part, this was due to a newly emerging viewpoint of Malcolm X, which lay at the core of his coming split with his patron and leader Elijah Muhammad. It seemed clear that Malcolm X, whatever he had previously believed, was now moving to a broader analysis of the race problem and laying the ground for some collaboration with those, both black and white, whose views were not those of his so-called Islamic creed.

I quickly perceived what had attracted Handler to this man. Handler was a student of Marxism. He knew all of the revolutionary thinkers: Marcuse, Sorel, Hegel, Herzen, Trotsky, Berdayev, Mill, Chernyshevsky, Plekhanov. He was an admirer of French logic and German philosophy. He detected in Malcolm X a mind that approached social, economic, and political questions with hard-edged reasoning, in sharp contrast to the softer, more emotional thinking of the black and white elites of the civil rights movement for which Malcolm X had expressed contempt, perceiving in it subservience, white superiority, and black inferiority.

To be certain, Malcolm X's rhetoric had been marked by its own emotionalism, the appeal to black nationalism, inspiration of hatred, *fierce* hatred, for those forces, specifically white, on whom he placed the burden of guilt for subordination and depersonalization of blacks.

Handler was right. There was a cutting edge to the mind of Malcolm X. He was relentlessly sawing away at the superstructure of rhetoric and cant that had almost buried a clear perception of the race question in America.

I have no recollection of whether we ate a meal or just consumed endless cups of very black scalding coffee. I left my first and only meeting with Malcolm X convinced that he was a *force*. How that force would play out I had no idea, but I felt certain that its context was changing and that this would change the landscape of the emerging race issue in America. I did not believe then (and I believe I am right) that Malcolm X had by any means come to the natural end of his life's journey and the continued evolution of his philosophy. Nor did I know how and where that life's journey had begun. Our talk was of the present and the future. The past got reference only in the debt that it had left for the present to pay. I had no notion of what had led Malcolm X into the Nation of Islam, but I had a clear idea of what was leading him out. His mind had burst the restrictions of the concept of an Islamic state as a solution to the race problem. That, I thought, was a positive step.

Of his origins I knew little. I assumed he had been born in poverty simply because this was the background of so many black Americans. I did not know that he was largely self-educated and that as an adolescent he had passed through the nightmare of drug abuse, scams, hustling, pandering for black prostitutes, every kind of ghetto crime that afflicted young unemployed impoverished blacks. I had no notion that he had survived seven years in prison for burglary, theft, weapons possession, and that it was in prison he remade himself almost literally—abandoning the use of drugs, halting cigarette smoking, putting exploitation of women forever behind him, converting himself to a totally new diet, halting consumption of pork and halting excess in all forms—except, it could be said, excess in politics.

As I gradually became aware of Malcolm X's background, none of this surprised me because I had seen the force of his character. It never occurred to me on that spring evening that I should one day be writing about Malcolm X as an American folk hero. I confess the idea still seems farfetched. He was not *my* hero. To me, he was then and perhaps still is an *antihero*. But I understand it when he is written up as a cult figure, the epitome of the revolutionary ingredient that was carried within the great struggle to bring American practice somewhat more into line with American words, to make white Americans (and blacks) comprehend that the wonderful words of the Declaration of Independence, the Bill of Rights, and the post–Civil War constitutional amendments had never meant what they seemed to mean, that there still existed a black America beside a white America, a black America in every way underprivileged, never an equal at Democracy's table.

And as the years have gone by I have become convinced that it required someone like Malcolm X, with his fire, his intransigence, his impatience with excuses, any kind of excuse, to wake up the nation.

It was a rude awakening. Liberal Americans expected black Americans to thank them for supporting black rights. They did not see this as condescension. Malcolm X did. He did not think blacks had to tip their hats to obtain what was theirs by the majesty of the law. It was like thanking someone who was giving back to you the diamond he had stolen from your dressing table.

Malcolm X was a radical. It was no coincidence that he and Barry Goldwater shared a fondness for saying that extremism in the cause of the right was no sin.

Malcolm X had not been born with that steel in his backbone. That had been forged in life, and his life, like that of so many black Americans, had been lived in hate and fear. His home had been burned down when he was a child, not once but twice. Robed Klansmen had ringed the house and warned the family to get out of town. His father had died a violent and unexplained death, almost certainly murdered by racists who put the body across streetcar tracks, that it might be cut in two and appear as an accident. Malcolm was six at the time. Malcolm's mother looked like a white woman. Later Malcolm would say that he learned "to hate every drop of that white rapist's blood that is in me." Malcolm had a minimum of schooling and was hustling before he was sixteen. He would do anything for a buck. He was on drugs and had to earn money to support his habit. Naturally he peddled not only cocaine but women. He graduated from that to burglary, running his own gang and living the soft life of the grifter between jobs until, inevitably, he was busted in Middlesex County outside Boston and went up on a ten-year term of which he served seven years.

He was as disciplined as a member of the Queen's Lifeguards. He rose almost immediately to the side of Elijah Muhammad and became the official spokesman of the Muslims, articulate, firm, stern, severe, not deviating one inch from Elijah's creed. He was a phenomenon, and soon press and TV reporters buzzed around him. He was the rage of the talk shows, unsmiling, with round steel-rimmed glasses, a black Savonarola.

He moved onto the international scene, visiting Mecca, traveling to Muslim countries and to the black republics of Africa, an international statesman and a black superstar, never permitting a finger's width to distance his words from those of Elijah.

But beneath his cool there was a caldron of conflict. Elijah Muhammad's republic throbbed with intrigue. A hundred figures vied for favor, and all united against Malcolm X. It was apparent that when and if Elijah Muhammad entered the promised land of Allah, Malcolm X would inherit the kingdom.

The House of Islam was not a tidy kingdom. Its members had emerged from the bitter underclass. There were bodyguards (called the Fruit of Islam) and, it was said, hit squads. At intervals members died violent and mysterious deaths.

The danger came not alone from within. Malcolm X's stark views brought him the hatred of the backers of Klan and white supremacy groups. He moved with a bodyguard himself. When he was in a public place he always took a chair facing out, as he did the evening we met in the Muslim restaurant. If an enemy were to appear, he would be ready. Did he go armed? It would have been common sense.

Against this background Malcolm moved up in the black movement. He was a lone player, but he aroused strong passions. About the time I met him, a breach had developed between himself and his leader. Malcolm had acquired new ideas in his foreign travels. His horizon had widened. He had found, for example, that by no means all Muslims were dark in hue, as he had supposed. Many were blue-eyed, blond-haired, fair-skinned. Color alone was not the key. This simple observation brought profound readjustments in his thought.

Malcolm had begun to say he had learned the real truth in Mecca. He began to make remarks that were anathema to his early Black Muslim declarations. His dearest friends, he said, now "have come to include all kinds, Christians, Jews, Buddhists, Hindus, agnostics, atheists . . . black, brown, red, yellow and *white*! [his italics]"

His breach with Elijah Muhammad involved questions of principle, but there were questions of practice as well. Malcolm discovered that Elijah had had relations with two of his secretaries and that each had borne a child by him. When Malcolm X confronted Elijah, the leader suspended him. An open break quickly followed. Malcolm now denied that Elijah was, in fact, Allah's Messenger, declaring that the last true Messenger had appeared in Mecca 1,400 years before.

A year after our conversation Malcolm went public with his apostasy. He launched his own organization of Afro-American Unity, drawing members from Muhammad's Nation of Islam. The Sunday before he made the announcement Malcolm came to Handler's apartment and discussed his plans.

By now Handler was no longer writing about Malcolm X in the *Times*. A new city editor, A. M. Rosenthal, had forbade mention of Malcolm X in the paper. To Rosenthal, he was as much a demon as Malcolm had perceived the white man as being. Handler maintained his link to Malcolm in secret but soon was railroaded into retirement.

Malcolm seemed to Handler like a man who had reached a crossroads and was making a choice under inner compulsion. "A wistful smile illuminated his countenance from time to time," Handler recalled. Handler sensed that Malcolm was not certain he would succeed in escaping the shadowy world in which he had existed. Handler's wife thought Malcolm had the look of a panther seeking a new path.

It was not long before Malcolm began to talk of his mortality, of death. He told Alex Haley, his biographer, "If I am alive when this book comes out . . ." One day he said, "I'm a marked man." He got telephoned death threats. Police escorts began to appear. His own bodyguards now carried shotguns. Sightings of hostile Black Muslim groups, some openly armed, were reported. Malcolm X made a trip to Los

Angeles January 26, 1965. Black Muslim groups followed him to his hotel, loitered there, then followed him back to the airport. He appeared on a TV show in Chicago and told of attempts on his life.

Malcolm X flew to Selma, Alabama, for a rally in late February and then to Paris, where he was barred from landing, and on to London, returning to New York February 13. The night after his return his home was firebombed. He managed to save his pregnant wife, Betty, and four children. Half the house was burned down.

He telephoned Alex Haley, canceling a planned interview, saying, "I have been marked for death in the next five days." He met with photographer Gordon Parks February 18, a Thursday. Parks asked if it was true that killers were hunting him. "It's as true as we are standing here," he replied.

On Saturday afternoon, February 20, Malcolm X checked into the New York Hilton hotel, parking his blue Oldsmobile in the hotel garage. He left his twelfth-floor room only to dine at the Bourbon room. Sunday morning he telephoned his wife and suggested that she and their four children come in from their Long Island home to the Audubon Ballroom between Broadway and St. Nicholas on West 166th Street, just north of the Audubon cemetery where many of New York's most famous nineteenth-century citizens are buried, across the street from the American Academy of Arts and Letters.

Malcolm checked out of his Hilton room at noon, had the bellman bring his car to the entrance, got in, and drove uptown to the Audubon. There were 400 wooden chairs set up for his talk. Malcolm rejected any security check of the audience. "If I can't be safe amongst my own kind," he said, "where can I be?"

He got to the Audubon a bit ahead of time. Several reporters were present. He spoke briefly to them. He wore a dark suit, white shirt, and dark tie. He paced the dressing room a bit and started talking about the bombing of his home. He had been, he said, possibly hasty in blaming the Black Muslims. He had heard things that suggested some other agency was to blame. "The way I feel," he said, according to Haley, "I ought not go out there today."

A young aide, Benjamin Goodman, gave a warm-up speech, then introduced Malcolm. He listened from the side of the stage and walked out with a smile as Goodman concluded. The applause swelled. Malcolm X greeted the audience: "*Asalaikum salaam! Asalaikum salaam*, brothers and sisters!"

At that point a disturbance broke out about eight rows from the front. A man yelled: "Take your hand out of my pocket!"

Malcolm X stepped forward, shouting: "Hold it! Hold it! Don't get excited. Let's cool it, brothers."

As Malcolm spoke, as the audience craned its necks to look back to the outburst, three men arose in the front rows and opened fire. A reporter saw two men run toward the stage, one with a shotgun, one carrying two revolvers. Another reporter said Malcolm was shot with his hands still raised in the air to still the crowd. One man running backward kept firing at Malcolm, his gun half-concealed by his jacket.

Malcolm X's hand, Haley reported, clutched at his chest. Sixteen slugs hit his body. His other hand flew up. Blood gushed from his chest. He fell dead, knocking over two chairs, his head hitting the stage with a thump.

His wife, Betty, made her way to her husband, prone on the platform. "They killed him!" she cried. Malcolm was rushed to Columbia-Presbyterian emergency room a block and a half distant. He was dead on arrival at 3:15 P.M.

On March 11, 1966, Thalmadge Hayer, twenty-two, Norman 3X Butler, twenty-six, and Thomas 15X Johnson were convicted of first-degree murder in the death of Malcolm X. They were sentenced to life imprisonment. The three were members of the Black Muslim temple in Paterson, New Jersey.

8

The Family of Liu Shaoqi

NOT EVERY MEMBER of this family is a hero and some are more heroic than others, but one thing is certain: no one in my pantheon shines more brightly than Wang Guangmei, Liu's widow.

I met Wang Guangmei on a brilliant October day beside Behai Lake in the Forbidden City. We lunched in an ancient restaurant that serves the miniature dumplings that her chef invented to divert the taste of the empress dowager when she was fleeing Peking to escape the Allied troops seeking revenge for the Boxer uprising in 1900. The room in which we lunched was still decorated in imperial yellow.

We could have been dining in Paris—exquisite service, white-jacketed waiters, elegant cuisine, and my hostess whose style would have blended imperceptibly among the strollers on the Rue St. Honoré.

I had seen photographs of the obscene charade staged by Mao's Red Guards, Madame Wang dressed as a "bourgeois

74

queen" with a necklace of Ping-Pong balls around her throat and her figure jammed into a mock *qipao* (the traditional Chinese dress), skirt slashed to her thighs, Mao's teenagers dancing about and shouting like red devils.

I knew from Wang Guangmei's daughter, Pingping, how her children had rescued her from Qincheng prison, a year after Mao's death, she a living skeleton, so dazed with torture and deprivation she could hardly talk, not comprehending that she again saw the sun and breathed air not fetid with the stench of rotting bodies.

Now I was talking with this woman, her face beautiful, her smile dazzling, her mind agile and witty as though she had spent her life in the salons of Marcel Proust.

I could not bear to hear the tale she told, of the suffering inflicted on her husband, Liu Shaoqi, the president of China and Mao's anointed heir, and the savaging of her children. Even their faithful old cook spent six years in prison for having prepared meals for "a traitor family."

Listening to this sparkling woman, returned from the shores of Lethe, I began finally to perceive the depths of madness into which Mao Zedong had plunged China, and I knew that I would never know a family equal in courage to that of Liu Shaoqi.

They had lived in Mao's pleasure gardens of Zhongnan-hai, in a corner of the Forbidden City, sealed for centuries against the eyes of outsiders. Their palace was called Fu Lu Ju, the House of Good Fortune. It had been used by the ill-fated son of the empress dowager for festive gatherings and particularly for birthday celebrations. It was a calm and peaceful life, Liu Shaoqi so busy he seldom had much time for his family. His wife remembered Mao spending more time playing and joking with the children than their father. Yang Shangkun, president-to-be of China, bought them ice cream cones or took them to the movies. Zhongnanhai seemed a quiet neighborhood, friends dropped in, walking from palace to palace. On Sundays all promenaded around the lakes.

Imperceptibly this began to change in 1966 with the onset of Mao's Great Proletarian Cultural Revolution. Peace and repose were broken by shouts and tumult. To the Liu children, especially the two oldest, Pingping and her brother, Yuanyuan, these were confusing but exciting days. Like all high school youngsters, they joined Mao's Red Guards, wore red kerchiefs around their necks, and went to demonstrations, shouting against enemies of Mao. They took excursions into the countryside to attack what Mao called the "Four Olds," old ideas, old culture, old customs, and old habits.

Big-character posters called *dazibao* began to appear, attacking a litany of "enemies." The children walked through the familiar lanes of Zhongnanhai reading the posters, coming home to tell their parents about them. Liu tried to explain the Cultural Revolution to his children. He admitted he didn't understand it very well. "I've had no experience with Cultural Revolution," he said. "But I am studying it so I can help Chairman Mao."

Neither Liu nor the children suspected that Liu himself would emerge as Mao's chief target, the "Number One Capitalist Roader," accused of leading China away from communism and back to capitalism, helped by the "Number Two Capitalist Roader," Deng Xiaoping.

Liu told his children that he and Deng had asked Mao how to carry out the revolution, but Mao was not helpful. He told them to act on their own. Not until the summer of 1966 did the children begin to suspect there was something odd about their father's situation. He no longer was busy with state affairs. He went to his office in a wing of their palace, but his in-and-out baskets were always empty. One day the children came home to tell Liu they had seen a *dazibao* attacking him personally. Incredibly, not until August, when

Mao himself wrote a *dazibao*, did China's president finally realize that it was he, Liu Shaoqi, who was the bull's-eye of Mao's assault. Neither Liu nor his wife imagined what lay ahead. The children could not grasp the ring of terror that was tightening about them and their parents. One day "Auntie" Cai Chang, a very, very old friend of Mao's, a prominent woman leader, and Zhongnanhai neighbor, stopped eleven-year-old Tingting on the street and asked about her mother. "Oh," said Tingting, "she is fine. She is selling food at the students' dining hall at Qinhua University." Cai Chang burst into tears. "Oh, you silly child," she exclaimed. "You still don't know anything."

One evening Pingping and Yuanyuan announced at the dinner table that they were going out with their fellow Red Guards to the house of a prominent neighbor and search it for "Olds." Their father was appalled. "Don't go," he said. He took from his bookcase a compilation of China's laws. He told the children it was all right to follow Mao's command to destroy the "Four Olds" but not to search and confiscate private property or to beat people. "I am the president," he said, "and I am responsible for the laws of this country."

Their father's words made an impression. The children never went on another confiscation mission. Slowly they began to perceive what was going on. Liu Shaoqi met with the Party Central Committee and wrote a self-criticism in which he tried to take blame for "his faults." Mao himself approved Liu's statement. "It is well-written," he scribbled on the document, "especially the last part."

The family thought their troubles were over. They weren't. Jiang Qing and the Gang of Four circulated the self-criticism all over the country, snipping off Mao's comment. It was used to arouse "a high tide of criticizing Liu." Liu went to Zhou Enlai and proposed that he resign and take all blame on himself. He would retire to the countryside and become a farmer. This would end the disruption of the country and relieve his thousands of associates who were being tormented. Zhou said he was sorry but Liu would not be allowed to resign. The madness rose higher and higher. Mao's oldest associate, Marshal Zhu De, began to be attacked as "a black commander" and "warlord." None of the heroes of Mao's revolution was safe from attack.

Liu called in his children. He took some papers from his desk and let them read them. He showed them Mao's approval of his self-criticism. He showed them documents exposing the falseness of every charge against him. And he revealed that not once since he had become president of China had Mao ever signed or vetoed a single act taken by Liu. He merely put a tiny circle in red pencil to indicate he had seen the decree. He never said yes. He never said no.

Zhou Enlai warned Liu and his wife not to venture out of Zhongnanhai. Too dangerous. But one evening the telephone rang. A voice said that Pingping had been hurt in a car accident. She had to have an operation. They hurried to the hospital. It was a trick. Pingping was not there. The Red Guards had set a trap to catch Wang Guangmei. Finally Zhou Enlai got her released. More and more the children were criticized and assaulted at school; even Tingting was persecuted by the "antireactionary" division of her grade school.

Late one night Liu got a call from Mao's secretary. Mao wanted to see him and sent his car. Once again Liu tried to resign and let all the blame be put on his shoulders in order to end the rising chaos. Mao smoked silently. Then he told Liu to go home and study several obscure Marxist works. "Study hard and take care of your health," he told Liu.

When Liu told his family, there was great relief. Everything was going to turn out all right. Mao had not criticized Liu. Two days later the Red Guards broke into the House of Good Fortune, plastered it with *dazibao*. They forced Liu and

Wang Guangmei to teeter on a desk lacking one leg while they raved and shouted. Next day Premier Zhou telephoned Wang Guangmei to warn: "Guangmei, you have to be strong. Get ready for the worst."

Liu's telephones were ripped out. He was ordered to cook his own meals, sweep the floor, and work by day instead of night as was his custom. They took away his sleeping pills. For days he did not sleep and came close to a total breakdown. He was taken to one "struggle" session after another. His hair turned white. Wang Guangmei was put before a shouting throng of 300,000 at Qinhua University in the mock garb of an empress, Ping-Pong necklace and all.

When Wang Guangmei finally struggled her way home, Liu called in the children and told them that he was certain he would be killed. He asked them to take his ashes and scatter them at sea as Friedrich Engels, Marx's associate, had ordered done with his. Wang Guangmei warned that the authorities would not give them the ashes. Liu insisted that they would. He said he would not commit suicide unless he was tortured to the edge of insanity. He asked the children to try to survive and go among the people, working for the future.

Wang Guangmei worried about Xiaoxiao, the six-year-old. If Wang Guangmei was arrested, would the authorities let her have Xiaoxiao in prison with her as Chiang Kaishek had let Communist women take their infants to prison with them? Liu did not think so, and Wang Guangmei turned Xiaoxiao over to her nurse, gave the nurse pictures of Xiaoxiao's parents, and charged her with the child's safety. Already several relatives of Liu, including a son and daughter by his first wife, had fallen victim to the Red Guards.

On August 5, 1967, Liu Shaoqi and Wang Guangmei were paraded before a mob of 100,000 at Tiananmen. Ping-ping, Yuanyuan, and Tingting were compelled to watch as their parents were carried in by armed guards, forced into the "airplane position" (hands firmly grasped from behind and heads bent in a low bow). The soldiers lifted Liu up and dropped him to the pavement in a jarring assault on his tortured body, kicking him, grabbing him by his white hair, and forcing him into contortions for the party photographers. Suddenly a wild cry cut the air. It was six-year-old Xiaoxiao who had been brought to the meeting. The crowd quieted. Yuanyuan ran toward her. Soldiers tried to halt him. He brushed them away, shouting: "Can't you see Xiaoxiao is crying?"

Liu and his wife were beaten until blood ran from their faces, shoeless feet bruised and bleeding, forced to bow to portraits of Mao. Wang Guangmei reached out and clasped her husband's hand. They stood silently staring into each other's eyes as the guards kicked and struggled to tear them apart. It was their farewell. The children were carted into prisons, beaten along with the children of other leaders— "uncles" as they called Deng Xiaoping, Peng Zhen, Lin Feng, Bo Yibo, Yang Shangkun, and Luo Ruiqing.

They had to fend for themselves if they were released from custody. Yuanyuan and the son of Peng Zhen sold their blood to a hospital to get money to eat. The second time they went to give blood they were turned away. Theirs, the hospital said, was "black blood." Pingping was beaten at school because she put newspapers under her thin blanket to keep warm. One paper had a photo of Mao. She was accused of demeaning the great chairman. The children scattered over the countryside, working in fields along the Yellow River, their lives saved by kindly peasants.

Pingping remembered an old soldier putting his arm around her and saying: "you are good children of your father. Stay alive for your father." One by one, with endless difficulty, often caught and returned to the countryside, they slipped back into Beijing. Of the fate of their parents, they had no notion.

They did not know that their father, crying endlessly in an autonomic fit, emaciated from starvation, torture, and lack of medical treatment, his hands clutched in spastic claws, had been secretly flown out of Beijing to Kaifeng, naked, feeding tubes in his nose, thrust into a cement-floored cell, and left there to die at 6:00 A.M. November 12, 1969, his hair uncut, a matted gray beard, his face sunken, a mass of bruises, unrecognizable. The burial certificate gave his name as Liu Weihuang; occupation, none; cause of death, disease. Not for three years did the children learn of the death.

On the eighteenth of August, 1972, they were allowed to visit their mother in Qincheng prison, her hair gray and stringy, hardly able to stand, wearing an old army coat, her face blank and sunken. She did not know, nor did the children tell her, that Lin Biao had sentenced her to death, her life saved only because when Zhou Enlai came to Mao with the signed death warrant Mao exclaimed: "Save the prisoner and spare the knife"—an old Chinese proverb. Zhou had exclaimed: "Oh, Chairman Mao, you are so generous!"

The children did not tell her of Liu's death or of the death of her eighty-year-old grandmother in the same Qincheng prison.

The search of the children for the ashes of their father started that day. It went on and on. They asked his old bodyguards. They found soldiers who had guarded him in Kaifeng. They asked at Babaoshan, the place where the remains of leaders are cremated and the ashes preserved.

Not until 1976, after Mao's death, did they get a clue. The ashes might be in a room at Babaoshan in an unmarked box. They went to the room. In the center they found the ashes of Kang Sheng, Mao's secret police agent, in a spittle-stained box covered with the red-and-gold flag of China.

Nearby was an unmarked box containing ashes. No way to know whether they were those of Liu Shaoqi or another victim of the madness. The children took a handful of ashes, and on September 30, 1976, three weeks after Mao's death and the day before the twenty-seventh anniversary of the People's Republic of China, they made their way to Tiananmen. There in the waters of the Golden River, which flows in a marble channel before the Imperial City, they scattered the ashes, in fulfillment of Liu's last wish, that his ashes be scattered like Engels's in the sea. By many convolutions the waters of the Golden River flow into the Yellow River and then into Bohai gulf.

Not until Deng Xiaoping came into power was Wang Guangmei released from prison, to reappear in Chinese society as svelte as the day she left it, to resume her position as a leading figure in the ranks of China's ruling circle, a voice for frankness, for dedication to her country, for honesty, with a keen sense of China's future, and the central figure of a family conscious of its destiny and its obligation to China.

Once again the surviving children gathered with their mother in Beijing to discuss the roles they would undertake. It had always been a rule of Liu Shaoqi that each was to express his or her opinion honestly and without reserve. Children should not be forced into careers; they should select their own way of service to the state.

The most dramatic decision was that of Yuanyuan. He opted to return to the grass roots of Henan, to work with the peasants who had saved his life. For years he worked, the only member of his class at Beijing University to elect to work in the country, not in the capital. He worked in a commune with men and women who had no notion he was Liu's son. He put his knowledge of mathematics and engineering to their use in solving problems of drainage and irrigation. He was one of them. When his secret was finally disclosed, more than

one peasant warned him: "You are too honest. You can never have a political career unless you are willing to tell lies."

Yuanyuan did not change his style. He rose rapidly in provincial work to the rank of vice-governor. There it seemed that, indeed, his reputation for honesty might slow his advance. But he did not compromise. His oldest sister went to Columbia University in New York and became a nutrition specialist, selecting her specialty because she felt that feeding China was *the* problem of the future. She went back to join Beijing municipality and begin to oversee its nutritional needs.

The younger sisters, educated in the United States and Germany, entered careers in banking and finance, determined to devote their lives to lifting their country out of its often medieval economy. There were not a few in China who looked to the political futures of Yuanyuan and his sister Pingping as symbols of the generation that hoped to lead China toward a new plateau of development and participatory government in the years beyond the reign of Deng Xiaoping. No family in China had been so tested by trial and torture. No family had emerged with a firmer determination to make China a place where the horror of the past should not be repeated.

9

Nikita Sergeyevich Khrushchev

IN THE CHILLY OCTOBER TWILIGHT of 1960 Nikita Khrushchev was chatting with reporters at the handsome iron gates of the Glen Cove estate of the Soviet Mission to the United Nations on Long Island.

It had been a long dull Sunday, and he had enlivened it by occasionally walking up to the gates and bantering with the handful of reporters on duty there.

As dusk fell he came to the gates once more, ordered them opened, and we went in for a more leisurely conversation. I had been following Khrushchev for several years both in Russia and the United States. I had been with him when he made his famous visit to Roswell Garst's farm in Coon Rapids, Iowa, and sat in the United Nations gallery and watched him lean down, pull off his shoe, and start banging on the table to show his disapproval.

I liked Khrushchev. Most politicians, Russians and American alike, are flawed, and Khrushchev was no exception. But he had a small boy's curiosity and naïveté which drew me to him and him to me. We trusted each other—up to a point. Khrushchev was good newspaper copy because he did and said the most unlikely things. Never a dull day with him. When he went to Belgrade to apologize to Marshal Tito for Stalin's attempt to topple him, he got falling-down drunk. When he was in Washington, he refused to go up in a helicopter until Ike agreed to go with him because he had never been in a helicopter and thought the CIA might drop him over the side. In the days when he was an illiterate coal miner (he didn't learn to read until his early twenties), he heard some people at the boardinghouse mention ballet. As he confessed, he didn't know what they were talking about— maybe something to eat, a strange kind of fish.

When Khrushchev decided to attend the UN General Assembly in New York in 1960, he sailed aboard the dingy Soviet steamer *Baltika*, but because he feared the CIA might torpedo his ship he made the heads of the satellite states come too. He didn't think the United States would sink the whole gang.

Khrushchev had a snub nose, little pig's eyes, enough energy to run a power generator, and a born politician's instinct for word and gesture. When he stood in front of a Hollywood audience and told how he had been banned from going to Disneyland, you saw the tears form in the corners of his eyes. When he chose to feel insulted by the Los Angeles mayor, you could see the lightning flash as he talked of going home where the Soviet bomber fleet awaited. When he saw the magnificent corn and fat pigs of the Garst farm, you could see him ache with envy that the Ukraine did not possess such corn and pigs.

Khrushchev appreciated good workmanship, and he was quick to pick up the difference between hands-on reporting and the Russian kind in which writers seldom left their offices to see what they were writing about. I was on the sidewalk outside his Sixty-eighth Street residence at 6:00 A.M. every morning, and I was still there until he went to bed after midnight. He saw and appreciated that kind of work. I think, too, that he was impressed to see me crawl under his feet and those of Richard Nixon during their kitchen debate so I could hear and record every word they exchanged.

I came to admire this roly-poly little man who was eager to inspect anything new (which had led him against his political inclination to follow Nixon over in the American home exhibitions to inspect the gleaming new kitchen equipment, having first dismissed it, saying, "We have all those things in my own kitchen.")

And I liked the attitude he displayed in Russia. When he went on a trip, he was always scrambling under counters to look at the drains and insisting on seeing the bathroom pipes. He knew shoddy Russian workmanship firsthand, and he crusaded endlessly against it. He was the first Russian commissar to begin to understand what Gorbachev proclaimed thirty years later—that communism didn't work. But Khrushchev still had hopes that by tinkering, the broken machine could be put back on the road. It was a vain hope.

I saw Khrushchev's curiosity lead him into a tour of the beautiful IBM building in San Jose, California, as the guest of Thomas J. Watson, Jr., who had no notion he was doing something revolutionary. The IBM facility was an example of a modern technological plant, an endless succession of cinderblock halls, one blending into another on a single level. Khrushchev started at the executive suite and moved into the general office section, along the assembly lines, into the shipping department, the warehouses, all the same building, all the walls pastel greens or pastel purples or pastel blues, all wall-to-wall carpeting, the same gentle piped-over background music, no lines of division. You couldn't tell whether you were in the director's office or the assembly line by the shape, contour, and ambience of the structure, the same casually dressed men and women whether they were vice presidents or on-line workers.

Halfway through the tour, I caught a glance exchanged between Khrushchev and one of his aides. They knew what Watson was showing them, even if Watson didn't. I knew, too, because I had read my Marx. I knew that the great goal of communism, and hence of the Soviet system, was to abolish the distinction between blue and white collar, between physical and mental labor, to wipe out the historic divisions between the "toiling" class and the "exploiting" class. I had been in hundreds of Soviet factories and knew their grim, back-breaking nature. The distinctions were far from gone in the Soviet Union. A blue-collar family would make any sacrifice to lift its sons and daughters out of the "toiling" ranks and into the white-collar bureaucracy. But here in America, in the citadel of capitalism, the historic distinctions of blue and white collar had been obliterated so completely that there wasn't a person in the IBM plant who knew what they were. No one in the IBM plant or among the Americans accompanying Khrushchev had any notion that they were walking through a chapter in Marx's forecast of the future.

That was the nuance that underlay the quick glance passed between Khrushchev and his aide, and it told me more about the Soviet Union and the distance that separated it from its aspirations than a thousand words. Capitalism had achieved Marx's goal and didn't know it; communism was so far distant from it that Khrushchev didn't dare talk about it.

When later Khrushchev proclaimed "We will bury you" and "Your children will live under communism," I knew that he was only whistling in the wind. He had to talk like that or admit, as Gorbachev did, that communism had failed, that there was no way in which the Soviet Union could catch up with capitalist America.

For all Khrushchev's faults, his braggadoccio, his clumsy attempts to blackmail Kennedy in the missile crisis, his blundering maneuvers against Mao Zedong, his instincts were not all bad. No man could have married a woman so straight and warm and intelligent as Nina Petrovna without a good heart. Nor possess a son so sympathetic, understanding—and realistic—as Sergei Khrushchev.

In evaluating the contradictions in Khrushchev's character, I never forgot Stalin and the terror. Khrushchev was Stalin's man, and Stalin saw to it that all his men dipped their hands in blood. Khrushchev had been ruthless. He had been guilty of crimes. Stalin imposed collective guilt on all those around him. But there was a difference between Khrushchev and, say, Lazar Kaganovich. Khrushchev had come to Stalin raw, ignorant, naive, ambitious. He possessed great energy and total belief that he was building a new and better Russia to replace the Russia into which he was born, a Russia so backward and cruel that when he finally read Zola's *Germinal* he thought it was about the mining village in which he and his father had labored.

Once Khrushchev entered Stalin's circle, there was never a moment in when he did not feel the breath of Stalin's paranoia. He understood, as he once whispered to Marshal Bulganin, that a man never knew when Stalin called him to the Kremlin whether he would go back home safely or wind up in the dungeons of the Lubiyanka. Khrushchev played the role of a clodhopper as self-protection. He was Stalin's fool. As he once said, if Stalin asked him to dance the *gopak*, a bone-jarring Ukrainian dance, "I danced the *gopak*." If Stalin told a joke, Khrushchev laughed. If Stalin slipped a rotten tomato on the seat of his chair, Khrushchev sat down firmly, wetting his pants, and joined in Stalin's roar of glee. Khrushchev played the game—and survived.

Periodically, Khrushchev indulged in drunken displays of vicious vituperation—none worse than the spectacle he created at the Kremlin in the winter of 1963 when he invited writers and artists to a reception. For hours he heaped ugly abuse on them, particularly the poet Andrei Voznesensky. "You tell lies!" Khrushchev shouted. "You think you are a genius. We won't put you in prison but the frontier is open."

Most of the men around Stalin lost every vestige of humanity. It was not quite true of Khrushchev. When the day came and he could speak up, he spoke. In his famous "Secret Speech" he detailed crime after crime committed by Stalin. True, the list was not complete. Some crimes against party associates were not listed, some that affected Soviet foreign relations. But Khrushchev tore the veil of secrecy from Stalin's terror and exposed the ugly body of Soviet rule as not even its most violent opponents had been able to do.

Like all politics, this was not only moral outrage. There was political advantage. Khrushchev's opponents had dipped their hands far deeper into blood than had he.

All this was in Khrushchev's mind as he talked with me on that autumn evening at Glen Cove. I had said that many American politicians admired him as a professional and some had suggested he would have been very successful with the American voters. He acknowledged that he had heard such talk. If he had been an American politican, he said, he would have led the voters to communism. Then he went on to talk of the art of politics in the Soviet Union. "You have no idea, Mr. Salisbury," he said, "how hard it is to be a politician. There is no harder job on earth." He gave the impression that he never had a moment of ease. At any moment he might be confronted by a plot to overthrow him.

This cunning man, trained by life under Stalin never to

take anything for granted, was badly weakened by a totally unexpected source—Eisenhower. Khrushchev had come to regard Eisenhower as a man of peace, an honorable man in a world of savages. He had given Ike his trust in an endeavor to lay a basis for world peace. The two would meet at Paris in the spring, then on to Russia where Ike would be Khrushchev's guest, as Khrushchev had been Ike's in America.

Khrushchev was as happy as a small boy. He rushed back to Moscow to prepare. He had surprises in store for Ike. He would build a golf course in the Crimea (there was none in Russia); he himself would take lessons so he could accompany Ike. He would erect a beautiful villa overlooking Lake Baikal where Ike could be entertained in Siberia. And, most grandiose, he would build "Soviet-Land," a Russian version of Disneyland—all for Ike and to celebrate an accord of mutual trust and peace between the superpowers.

It was not to be. On May 1, 1960, Soviet antiaircraft gunners shot down Gary Powers, piloting a U-2 plane of the CIA over Sverdlovsk. The flights had been going on for a couple of years, as both Khrushchev and Ike well knew. Ike signed off on the May 1 flight with no inkling that it might destroy the peace drama he and Khrushchev had put together.

When word of the downing of the U-2 reached Moscow, Khrushchev sought out the American ambassador, Llewelyn (Tommy) Thompson, at a diplomatic reception. "You have to help me," he told Tommy. "I'm in a terrible spot." It was not the first time the Communist boss had come to the American ambassador for help. Tommy understood Khrushchev's position. The hard-liners would try to torpedo peace. He said he would do everything he could.

What Khrushchev needed was a repudiation by Ike of the spy flight. But Ike, acting the role of a loyal commander, refused to duck responsibility. He had signed off on the flight. He was responsible. That blew it. The Paris meeting turned into an angry shambles; Khrushchev withdrew Ike's invitation. The golf clubs were mothballed; "Soviet-Land" was never completed. The magnificent villa on Lake Baikal was turned over to Intourist to house VIPs.

Never, Khrushchev once said years after his fall, did he regain the power he held before the U-2 incident. He was fatally weakened.

I think Khrushchev dramatized the effects of the U-2 a bit. But it did mark a turning point. Not long after that I talked with him; he was in a philosophical mood. He spoke of Nixon. He had a very unpleasant image of Nixon, Nixon was such an anti-Communist. He could hardly have imagined that Nixon one day would lead the United States into détente and the cooling of the cold war. And long after Kennedy, Eisenhower, Khrushchev, Brezhnev, and all the players were gone, Nixon would live on to try to bring sanity into President George Bush's "We won–they lost" attitude toward Russia.

Russians, I realized, had as much trouble understanding American policy as Americans did Russian.

This misunderstanding was implicit in Khrushchev's talk about how difficult it was to deal with Americans. "Now," he said, "if you were president of the United States I could deal with you without difficulty. You are honest and aboveboard. I know where you stand."

I thanked him for the compliment, but I thought that his lack of background had led him to a false conclusion. Certainly, I tried to write about Khrushchev honestly. I did not indulge in Communist bashing. But did he understand that it was possible to write objectively about him without sharing his viewpoint? *Pravda* operated on the old Lenin principle of political polemics ("First we put the convict's badge on him, then we consider his case"). In the *New York Times* we stated Khrushchev's case and let our readers make up their own minds.

Still I gave Khrushchev high marks. He had come up from nowhere. He had tasted the heady delights of power and emerged to lead one of the great countries of the world. He led it with greater skill than his predecessors and with regard for the welfare of his people. He possessed a sense of realism which underlay his excitable curiosity. He could and did change his mind and admit it publicly.

I believe Nikita Sergeyevich Khrushchev was a flawed politician, but the important thing was not his flaws but his virtues. He was a bit like Fiorello La Guardia. He committed terrible blunders. But when he saw what he had done, he had the courage to admit it.

After he retired, Khrushchev invited Neizvestny to his dacha and apologized for his words. Following his death—at his specific wish—his widow commissioned Neizvestny to design the simple monument that stands at his grave in Novodeviche cemetery.

In retirement, Khrushchev for the first time had leisure to read. He read everything Mikhail Sholokhov had written. Sholokhov had been his literary hero. When he finished his reading, he told his family: "The son of a bitch! He's written only one novel, *The Quiet Don*."

When Pasternak's *Doctor Zhivago* appeared in the West and Pasternak was awarded the Nobel prize, Khrushchev led the attack that resulted in Pasternak's expulsion from the Writers' Union.

Now, Khrushchev read *Doctor Zhivago*. When he had finished, he burst out in a stream of Russian *mat*, that primitive Russian profanity constructed around the mother oath. "Damn it," he said (his actual words were more bawdy). "Those bastards simply fooled me. They told me this was a terrible book, an anti-Soviet work, that it befouled our revolution. They were just lying. There is nothing wrong with *Doctor Zhivago*. Sure, we might have cut a word or two—so what? To create an international furor over this book and hold us up to ridicule and denunciation all over the world—it is just impossible."

On one of the first days of September, 1971, Yevgeny Yevtushenko got a telephone call to come to the Khrushchev villa. It was a fine day, with sunshine and the scent of autumn in the air. Zhenya, as he told me, found Nikita Sergeyevich, Nina Petrovna, Khrushchev's son Sergei, and his daughter Rada there. They sat on benches in the garden and talked almost all day. Khrushchev had been ill and in the hospital, and he felt his end was approaching. He wanted to apologize to Yevtushenko and to the other writers he had criticized. He wanted to explain what had happened. When Yevtushenko had spoken to him in 1962, he had known that Yevtushenko was right.

"Then why did you shout at me, Nikita Sergeyevich?" Yevtushenko asked.

"Because I knew you were right," Khrushchev replied, "and I had to shout. You are very lucky. You are a poet. You can tell the truth. But I was a politician. You don't know what a terrible job it is to be a politician. I had to shout to hold my job."

Those bastards, said Khrushchev, referring to the party apparatchiks. The *svolochi!* They did not know what the revolution was about. "We gave birth to them," said Khrushchev, "and they will kill us."

For hours, Khrushchev spoke with the poet he had once criticized. He went back over the events of his life, the tasks he had carried out for Stalin. Finally, they went inside and had a meal. It was dusk when Yevtushenko left the dacha, tired and drawn, tremendously moved by Khrushchev's talk. It was his *Areopagitica.*

A week later, Yevtushenko's telephone rang again. It was Rada, the Khrushchev daughter: "Poppa died." Yevtushenko went to the service at the Kuntsevo funeral home. There were about fifteen members of the Khrushchev family, a few others: Sergo Mikoyan, son of Anastas Mikoyan, who brought a wreath from his father; perhaps twenty persons outside the family. There were one hundred police on hand, another one hundred plainclothesmen. Across the street from the funeral parlor, a hundred curious people stood, women with baby carriages, passersby. There was nothing to keep them from crossing the street. But no one did. Yevtushenko did not go on to the services at the cemetery. He was sick at heart and sick to his stomach. He went home and vomited.

No official of party or government attended the services. Thousands of police were on hand at Novodeviche cemetery, and only members of the family, a few diplomats, and correspondents were permitted to be present. His son Sergei spoke over the grave. "An honest and brave man has died," he said. I agreed.

10

Homer Bigart

NO NEWSPAPERMAN OF MY GENERATION so captured the admiration and envy of his colleagues as did Homer Bigart, a monosyllabic, unpretentious man with an irradicable stammer and a fierce tendency to scoop all of his competitors.

Homer was the best war correspondent of his times, which were, in fact, the age of wars—World War II, the Korean War, the Vietnam War, and conflicts of a more minor nature in other parts of the world.

I don't think there was a newspaperman I knew who did not respect Homer and wish that he possessed his cool grasp of a complex world and ability to report under fire with the clarity you might expect from someone recording the stately events of a formal dinner party. This did not mean that Homer did not feel fear as much as anyone—possibly more because he had seen so much of it, had seen so many men, including his colleagues, die in the grotesque manner of which death is a master.

Bigart and I arrived in wartime London about the same time in 1943, he in late January and I in early February. The only war I had known was the gang war in Al Capone's Chicago. I had lived in a third-rate hotel on Ohio Street in the Near North Side. I heard bombings every evening as the gangs demonstrated to cleaning shops that they needed its protection. My diet of reporting was largely gang killings, mob violence, and the depradations that made Chicago the liveliest town in the world. But I had never come under fire. Neither had Homer when he arrived to take up his assignment for the *Herald Tribune* in London.

It would be a mistake to call Homer the bravest man I ever knew. No man was more afraid of bullets than he. But he continued to report in spite of and in the presence of extreme danger. He once told me that he hated war but that you could not cover war without taking risks. The story was where the danger was. You could not stay back of the lines in a warm headquarters and write about the GIs in the trenches. That *was* the story. The front lines, the shudder of the ground when the big shells hit, and the whistle of the bombs as they fell and exploded close by.

Homer was a fine reporter before he came to World War II. He was a competitor. He had to get the story, and he had to get it first, and he had to have more of it than anyone else. He would not take second place. This nearly cost him his life during the Korean War because he was faced with an equally intense competitor, a woman willing to risk death for a scoop, a reporter on his own newspaper, Marguerite Higgins.

The relationship between Higgins and Bigart was deadly. Each sought positions more forward and more dangerous in order to outdo the other. There was no gentlemanly civility in Bigart's relationship with Higgins and no womanly courtesy on the part of Higgins. It was a duel to death or close to it.

There is no way, Bigart once said, in which he could justify his conduct toward Higgins. But, he added, he acted as he did because he thought she had deliberately caused him to expose himself to sudden death.

No one was farther from the Richard Harding Davis stereotype of a war correspondent than Homer. It is true that he wore a trenchcoat, but he never wore one with the collar turned up. He never wore a pull-down felt hat. He wore a GI tin helmet. He eschewed the belted correspondent look. In rear areas he was compelled in World War II to wear the officer's garb of faintly pink trousers, olive drab jacket, and leather-visored cap, set off by a green armband marked with a "C" to designate him as a reporter. At the front he was to be found in a grubby windbreaker, scruffy pants, and the tin hat. He did not play games with shell fragments.

The reason my generation worshiped Bigart was for his total professionalism. No man was slower at writing a story. He drove us crazy with his meticulous questioning, asking the same question over and over in slightly different form. It was boring, but the next day when we saw his story we understood the repetition. Once Homer went out to the front with Neil Sheehan, a young reporter for the UP in Vietnam. It was three days of endless questioning of the commanders of the actions, even more tedious queries back at headquarters. It went on for three days, and Sheehan had not filed a single story. Neither had Bigart.

On the way back to Saigon on the third day, Neil threw up his shoulders. All that questioning, he said, and no story. No story! Bigart responded with an exclamation point. No story! "Don't you understand? It doesn't work anymore."

What Homer had been establishing was the biggest story of all: the American intervention in Vietnam was no longer working; the planned battles were now frustrated by the Vietnamese; the U.S. firepower no longer brought victory;

the bombing did not halt the enemy. "It doesn't work anymore." That was it. No one but Bigart had noticed. Now by the most careful analysis and questioning, he had established the fact, years before America finally gave up.

Bigart was like that. When I first knew him in London, when we were both getting our first taste of war (not much of a war then, the blitz was over, London skies were more or less clear, preparations for European invasion were just getting under way), Bigart was honing his talents on the air war, the only one we had.

Each day he went to the big Ministry of Information press room on Malet Street and waited for the communiqué. He carefully questioned the briefing officers about every point, particularly the figures of plane losses, British and German. We all knew the figures were soft. The MOI used the biggest possible figure for Nazi losses and skimped on RAF casualties.

Then Bigart began the painful process of writing. He was always the last man out of the pressroom. Working for a morning paper in New York, he had no deadline worries; the six-hour time differential protected him. The image of Bigart that always comes to my mind is the sight of him—a slight, inconspicuous man—bending over his Olivetti typing one word at a time in the empty briefing room. There would be long pauses. He would skim through his notes again, look at the ceiling. He seemed totally unaware of whether the room was full or empty. There was never haste in his movements but always care.

Bigart went on the first U.S. daylight raid over Germany on which correspondents were permitted to accompany the B-17s. I was at the Molesworth base when the mission came back. Bigart was covering for the *Herald Tribune*, Robert Post for the *New York Times*, Walter Cronkite for UP, and Gladwin Hill for AP. It was a nervy moment. I was Cronkite's editor at UP and had been waiting for hours when the planes began to come back. Post's never made it.

All of the correspondents were uptight. The flak had been ferocious. Not a piece of cake. All had trouble getting their stories started. Bigart was slowest of all. Everyone had finished, and we waited and waited for Homer to join us in the command car which was to take us back to London where the dispatches would be filed. Finally he appeared, serious, unaware that his slowness had increased the tension among his fellow reporters. He was interested in only one thing— what did they lead with? Several had tried for grandiose effects, spotlighting the personal dangers of the mission. Bigart's lead was quiet, unemotional, effective, and complete: "Our target was Wilhelmshaven. We struck at Führer Adolf Hitler's North Sea base from the northwest after stooging around over a particularly hot corner of the Third Reich for what seemed like a small eternity."

No heroics. Just the facts.

Like any good correspondent, Bigart struck sparks with authority.

The first big blowup came with the Anzio landing in Italy. Homer had covered the Sicily operation and gone on to Italy. He knew the rudiments of military operations, and he knew the difference between fact and the protective fiction with which commanders surround an operation that goes bad. The Anzio operation was a disaster. Bigart went ashore with the troops and experienced every tragic moment.

He wrote the story, as much as he could get through the censor, and this brought down the wrath of Sir Harold R. L. G. Alexander, the commander. Alexander, in the pattern that has been typical of commanders since the time of Alexander the Great, blamed the correspondents, and especially Bigart, for the disaster. It was the messenger at fault, not the general. Bigart was not a mollycoddle. He struck back with blunter words, details, supporting his convictions. It was nip and tuck whether he would be expelled from Italy and placed on a slow boat for New York.

Better judgment finally prevailed at high command, but Bigart had established himself as a man who did not suffer personality puffs lightly.

It was in the Korean War that Bigart made his mark as the best war correspondent in the business. The Korean War of all those of the mid-twentieth century was the bloodiest, the most dangerous, the coldest, the most difficult, and, for a correspondent, the most lacking in reporting facilities. Bigart plunged ahead, sharing the frozen mud and the dangers with the troops, writing grim, mind-numbing reality. It did not endear him to the high command, but it won him respect from the troops. No creature comforts for Bigart, and he took no more shelter than they did. Bigart emerged from Korea in January, 1951, "the best correspondent of an embattled generation," according to *Newsweek*.

By the time Bigart reached Vietnam, going there first in the early days before massive American intervention, and then going back again as the American escalation got under way, he had seen more war than almost any of the commanders and had seen it more clearly and objectively. He had no taste for war, although he spent so large a portion of his life in it. He always regarded war as mean, ugly, distasteful—no positive qualities. He thought that it brought out the worst in those who participated. He did not make moral judgments, but nothing about war attracted him. He was suspicious of medals and heroes. He was a born reporter, and every reporter is a skeptic. Homer was brought up in western Pennsylvania, but he had the true Missouri spirit of "show me."

There was nothing in his background to suggest he was going to become the greatest reporter of his day. He had a conventional upbringing and came to New York where he caught on, rather late, as a copy boy for the *Herald Tribune*. It took him nearly five years to be promoted to chief copyboy and then to cub reporter. He was a slow starter, and he did not set the world afire with his talent. He was always a slow worker, and it took time for editors to realize that there was method in his slowness. His stories did not shine, as did so many of the *Herald Tribune* reports of that era, but they were always complete and to the point. Gradually he began to develop a style of his own, terse, no fancy effects, just the facts arranged in competent, complete detail with a tinge, just a tinge, of acerbity.

How he came to be sent to cover wars never was clear. He was respected in the *Tribune* city room, a tortoise to many *Tribune* hares, but a tortoise of a special kind.

In the 1950s Homer switched from the *Herald Tribune* to the *New York Times*. I think he always felt a bit uncomfortable about that. The *Times* had lured him with more money, and money was always important to him. It is likely, too, that fond as he was of the *Trib*, he perceived that it was not going to make it in the fierce competition with the *Times*. Homer did not like being number two.

Bigart was never number two on the *Times*. His achievements were the hallmark by which all other reporting was gauged, and he was a role model for every young reporter who joined the paper. Just to sit in the same city room with this owlish, solemn-faced man (a little fuller than in his war correspondent's prime) was an honor. He talked to the young reporters not like a father but like another reporter on the beat. He chafed with them about the city desk and the editors, calling the latter "those bastards" to their delight. He never let himself or the paper down in his copy, whether it was a trivial rewrite or the biggest scoop of the year. Bigart was solid gold, and everyone knew it. If some sloppy politician thought he could fob off Bigart with a conventional lie, he discovered his mistake quickly. Bigart's instinct for truth and his bulldog tenacity would bring the pol down in time for the first edition.

Homer died in 1991. An unusual assemblage of his peers and of young reporters for whom he was a legend gathered to give him tribute. Everyone in the room felt that he and his profession had been honored by the presence of this reticent man with the incurable stammer and the courage to place his life on the line to get the story.

Iphigene Ochs Sulzberger

IN THE WORDS OF BARBARA TUCHMAN, Iphigene Ochs Sulzberger was the best argument she could imagine for an elite class in American society—a woman "strong in conscience, in elegance of person and winning ways that gained her ends, in alert intelligence and irreverent humor, in energy and unfailing curiosity . . . a thoroughly delightful and thoroughly admirable person."

Iphigene Sulzberger was all that and more. She was an incorrigible pixie, a prankster, and under her gracious exterior lurked a rebel and sometimes a revolutionary. There were those—and I confess I was one of them—who saw her as the epitome of all that was good in the American dream. There were others, especially in the bizarre days of senators McCarthy and Eastland, who slyly hinted that she was a Communist agent and responsible for turning her father's good gray *New York Times* into what they called "the uptown edition of the *Daily Worker*," the Communist organ of the day. None, however, dared voice this slander openly, perhaps fearing reprisals from what could be the tartest tongue in town.

No one in later years was softer spoken than Iphigene, more gently tactful, but no one was quicker to pin a hypocrite down in the welter of his weasel words.

I have made many attempts to capture in words the surprise and delight of Iphigene Sulzberger. None were successful because capturing the essence of this remarkable woman is like trying to hold a rainbow in your hand. It is impossible.

In her last years Iphigene Sulzberger was the matriarch of one of America's great families. She had been since the death in 1935 of her father, Adolph Simon Ochs, the owner of the greatest newspaper in the world, a responsibility she carried on small but sturdy shoulders for nearly sixty years.

She did not rule with an iron hand, not even an iron hand encased in a velvet glove. She was a lady. When appropriate, she wore a lady's long white gloves fitted snugly up to her elbows. No metal, just a hand that was touch-sensitive, blood and flesh and nerves activated by a mind so swift it made a computer seem like a tortoise.

Iphigene was a prodigy. She knew it, but she never let anyone else know it. Or tried her best not to.

Once her magisterial father tried to invoke the hand of authority. Iphigene was six years old. Her father had taken her for a ride in an electric hansom cab from their flat on West Seventy-second Street to Grant's Tomb and back. Iphigene was tired and cross when they got home and refused to say good night to Mrs. Read, whose apartment they were renting.

Mr. Ochs took his daughter over his knee and spanked her. She screamed as loud as she could. She was outraged. Her father was violating her dignity. He was taking advantage of her because of her size. She hated him. She would never again, she screamed, have anything to do with him.

That was the first and last time the proprietor of the *New York Times* tried to discipline his daughter. Her declaration (as Iphigene remembered nearly eighty years later) took the spirit out of him. For three weeks he apologized and apologized, begging forgiveness. Finally Iphigene forgave her father, but, as she recollected with quiet glee, "from then on I had him wrapped around my little finger." She became a great lady in New York—and in the world. She rarely raised her voice after the outburst against her father. She didn't have to. At six she had learned how to use the levers that turn the wheels of society.

When her father died in 1935—and even for a few years before—Iphigene's quiet voice was the one that counted on the *New York Times*. She spoke so softly, penned her little notes so deftly (and wittily) that editors and businessmen never understood how her opinions so swiftly became their own.

Iphigene was the only child of Adolph Ochs, and her father spent as much time with his daughter as he did with the *New York Times*. Both became fabulous successes, successes so intertwined that no one, not even Iphigene, could untangle them.

With the death of her father Iphigene became the controlling voice in direction of the newspaper, but never in the years of her stewardship did she issue a direct order. Her first publisher was her husband, Arthur Hays Sulzberger. Her second was her son-in-law, Orvil Dryfoos. Her third was her son, Arthur Ochs Sulzberger. She never issued a directive to these men.

Iphigene did not believe in imposing her will. Often her husband, her son-in-law, or her son held opinions more conservative than hers. She did not protest. Sometimes they came around to her views, sometimes not, but her gentle hand kept the *New York Times* on the liberal-centrist course set by her father, upholding his sometimes fusty standards, moving slowly in the changing world but always fast enough to keep in tune with its times, not too far ahead, not too far behind.

Iphigene held to her father's precepts. The *Times* must be a pillar in the contentious world, a beacon from which people could take their bearings. Better be a bit late with a new style than to lead the readers into the morass of fool's gold.

The rebel in Iphigene Sulzberger was displayed at an early age. Her father entered her in Dr. Sachs's School for Girls. Dr. Sachs was authoritarian and Germanic. One day he lost his temper and delivered a violent rebuke to Iphigene's class. Dr. Sachs ordered her into his office. He thought she had been laughing at him. Iphigene listened in terrified silence until Dr. Sachs said: "What are you thinking about?" Ever truthful, Iphigene replied: "I think you have no business talking to me this way."

Dr. Sachs blew up. He called for Iphigene's governess and in Iphigene's presence called her a recalcitrant child. Iphigene couldn't stand it. She burst into tears and shouted: "He's a liar."

That did it. Iphigene was expelled from Dr. Sachs's classes.

It was Columbia College that brought Iphigene's rebelliousness into focus. She had classes under professors Benjamin Anderson, William Sheppard, James Harvey Robinson, and William Simkhovitch. She read Walter Lippmann, and she spent afternoons working at the Henry Street Settlement on the Lower East Side.

Iphigene began to think of herself as a socialist. (Communism had not yet been invented.) She dreamed of barricades and leading the mob against the cruel American capitalists.

Evening after evening she engaged her father in dinner table arguments about the injustice of the American system, about poverty and oppression. Adolph Ochs listened patiently. He plied her with questions. What was her authority? Who made that statement? He urged her to seek truth from facts. (Neither of them knew that Karl Marx had used that formula nor that it would be used later by Mao Zedong and Deng Xiaoping.) Seek Truth through Facts was the credo of Mr. Ochs's *New York Times*. He urged his daughter to follow it. Go back and check. Base your case on good source materials.

Iphigene did go back to the sources. All her life she would go back. It became the foundation of her dedication to history, especially American history, of efforts to improve American teaching of history, to a better understanding of the founding of the American republic. To the end of her days Iphigene passed it on to children, grandchildren, and friends—be sure of your facts. If you are not sure, look it up.

Her father put another tool for caution into Iphigene's hands. It was a saying that appeared on page 95 of Mr. Ochs's copy of Benjamin Franklin's autobiography: "I made it a rule to forbear all direct contradictions to the statement of others. I forbade myself the use of every word or expression that imported a fix'd opinion, such as *certainly, undoubtedly*, etc."

Thus, said Franklin, for fifty years he had avoided uttering a dogmatic opinion. Iphigene committed Franklin's words to memory. When her children pronounced some extreme statement, she had only to utter "Benjamin Franklin" to bring them down to earth.

She acquired two other maxims. One from Thomas Jefferson, her favorite founding father, was: "Always expect the best; you are no oftener wrong than when you expect the worst." And from James Harvey Robinson she picked an aphorism that served well in discussions with those who found her ideas on social progress impetuous: "Who ever heard of a vehicle going uphill that needed to have brakes applied?"

Iphigene's mind was crystal clear on issues of justice, racial equality, and a level playing field for the rich and the poor.

At an early age she had been taken to hear Booker T. Washington at Carnegie Hall because, as Mr. Ochs told his daughter, "he is a great man." It was the first time she had heard someone say that a black was a great man. This was in a day when President Theodore Roosevelt created a national uproar by inviting Booker T. Washington to lunch at the White House.

Iphigene's convictions had been influenced from the earliest times by the views of her grandfather, Julius Ochs. He abhorred slavery and wrote in his diary of the 1850s: "I saw attractive mulatto girls placed on the auction stand and subjected to a critical examination by lustful men. . . . Beatings and lashing with ugly thongs were frequent occurrences. These sights sickened me." Iphigene's grandmother, Bertha, was a rebel of a different sort. Bertha dipped her handkerchief into the blood of a fellow student executed in Germany's 1848 revolution. Her parents swiftly sent her to America, fearing she might suffer her classmate's fate.

Iphigene's mother was Iphigenia Wise, daughter of Rabbi Isaac M. Wise, founder of Reform Judaism in the United States. He had been forced to leave Germany after defying the government's restrictions on Jewish marriages (in an effort to hold down Jewish population). Rabbi Wise was a born rebel. He instructed the men in his first American congregation to remove their hats and the women to come down from the balcony and sit beside them. The congregation rose in anger. Wise narrowly escaped with his life. He refused kosher food. "My soul is not in my stomach," he said. Iphigene thought her grandfather's beliefs might have swept the Amer-

ican Jewish community had it not been for a wave of immigra-
tion of eastern European Jews, from the *shtetl* where they
lived in isolation, their medieval religious practices almost
unchanged. Iphigene's mother Iphegenia and her sister Helen
were educated at a convent school of the Sisters of Notre
Dame. The Roman Catholic archibishop asked Rabbi Wise if
he was not afraid that the Catholics would convert his daughters. Rabbi Wise replied: "Bishop, if you can convert those
girls after my teachings you are most welcome to have them."

The images to which Iphigene was exposed in her youth
afford clues to her nature. She was taken to see *Uncle Tom's
Cabin* more than once. It seared her mind with the brutality
of slave life. She saw in the Metropolitan Museum of Art the
painting of a beautiful Christian girl awaiting her fate in the
Roman amphitheater. She never forgot it. Nor did she forget
a painting of John Brown being led to his execution, hands
manacled behind his back, halting to kiss a black baby held
up by its mother.

The spectacle of the neglected, poverty-ridden children
in the slums around the Henry Street Settlement moved
Iphigene to tears. Seventy years later she could still feel her
flaming indignation against a society that permitted such evils.

She could not bear the reactionary editorials in her
father's paper and did her best to get him to turn the page
over to Walter Lippmann, darling of the progressives before
World War I. She got Mr. Ochs to agree to see Lippmann,
but the young *New Republic* editor refused to meet him.

This did not mean that Iphigene Sulzberger was prepared to lead the *New York Times* and its staff to the ramparts
once control of the institution fell into her hands. But it did
mean that a deep vein of social protest and rejection of bland
conservativism ran under her eminently proper matronhood.

She traveled the world, first with her father, then with
her husband, and after his death on her own. She knew the

moon was not made of green cheese. She saw the danger in Europe as Hitler rose to power, and she and her husband learned the reality of the Soviet dictatorship very early on. She didn't think much of General Eisenhower as president of Columbia University, and her opinion did not change when he became president of the United States. She liked Adlai Stevenson. Her husband and the *Times* supported Eisenhower in 1952, and she went along out of loyalty. In 1956 she voted for Stevenson, the man of her mind and heart.

Her father had never believed in Zionism. Nor had she and her husband. After the Holocaust she switched, giving up her idealistic dream of a Palestine in which Christians, Jews, and Muslims lived in peace.

Iphigene Sulzberger possessed a reflexive hatred for evil and cruelty. She was capable of picking a ladybug off a houseplant, opening the window, and letting it fly away home. She could not remain silent in the face of cruelty. She hated cant whether mouthed by a president or a priest. She had grave doubts about God. She enjoyed cross-examining intelligent men of religion—Jewish, Muslim, or Christian—about their God. Why did each suppose that his God was all supreme? How could each nation suppose that its God supported it when it warred on another? How could the God of the Jews permit the Holocaust?

She once told a rabbi at the Hebrew Union College that she did not think she was a true believer. She had too many doubts. The rabbi told her the essence of liberal Judaism was belief in the ethics of religion and keeping your mind open. He cited the prophet Micah who said, "What does the Lord require of thee but to do justly, and to love mercy and to walk humbly with thy God."

That satisfied her to a point, but she still could not feel certain about a personal God. "In the face of these mysteries," she said, "one should be humble."

A few years before her death in 1990 Iphigene dined with Zhou Enlai in Beijing. The premier ("probably to make conversation," she said) asked about her family. She told him it was large and diverse. There were Jews, Protestants, Catholics, and blacks. But no Chinese. What could she do about that—put an ad in the *People's Daily?*

Zhou smiled. No. The *People's Daily* didn't take ads. Well, said Iphigene, shall I put up a big-character poster in Tiananmen Square?

"Oh please," Zhou said, "don't do that. It would cause a riot."

It was a light conversation, but it had a serious subtext. Iphigene was telling the Chinese premier that America, despite its problems of race and religion, offered no social barriers to the mixing of color and creed. Both she and Zhou knew that despite its protestations these medieval qualifications still held sway in China.

When Iphigene Sulzberger died February 26, 1990, she left as a living monument the infusion of her principles and convictions not only into the paper her father had founded but, more important, into her own family, the owners, directors, and proprietors who far into the future would continue to maintain Adolph Ochs's *Times* as both an extraordinary economic enterprise and as a bulwark of democratic faith in an increasingly turbulent world.

12

Soong Chingling

THE GREAT LADY LAY DYING in the mansion she had inhabited for years, surrounded by sycophants, hangers-on, greedy retainers, cousins who had hurried in from across oceans and continents, two young wards, girls still in their teens, a heartbroken servant, a companion who had lived with the dying woman for half a lifetime.

The mansion was no ordinary residence. It had been built at the turn of the century, surrounded by gardens, a green English lawn, stout walls, and a massive gate. The surroundings spoke of wealth, power, prestige, and position.

This was not a chapter out of Zola or Trollope. The setting was Beijing in the thirty-second year of the People's Republic. The palace was that in which Henry Pu Yi, the last emperor, had been born in the old Manchu quarter beside the willows of Back Lake. Its great red lacquer door was guarded by a platoon of Communist soldiers quartered behind another red-lacquered gate next door.

The woman who was painfully living out her last days was the greatest in China, Soong Chingling, second daughter of Charlie Soong, the energetic Chinese who persuaded an American sailing captain to sign him on at the age of eight on a voyage to America. After apprenticeship to an uncle who ran a Boston grocery store, he launched a career that made him millions, earned first by peddling Bibles door-to-door in China and then as entrepreneur.

Soong Chingling was an unbelievably beautiful young woman when she married China's George Washington, Dr. Sun Yatsen, founder of the republic, on October 25, 1915, and she was still beautiful when I first met her fifty-seven years later.

She was twenty when she met Dr. Sun. He was forty-eight. She had been working as his secretary. He divorced his first wife and spirited Chingling off to Japan. Dr. Sun had been a paragon of Methodism. The marriage shocked Chinese Christians and the American missionary community. When in 1972 I met Madame Soong, seventy-seven, handsome and worldly, she was still sensitive to charges that Dr. Sun had divorced his wife to marry her. "He was already separated from her when we met," she insisted, calling stories of the divorce "Nationalist propaganda." She offered to show me her marriage certificate to prove she was innocent of breaking up Dr. Sun's first marriage.

She was sensitive on another point—her age. Our friendship almost foundered when she said I mistakenly made her two years older in a dispatch describing my dinner with her in the Henry Pu Yi palace. For years, so she said, the Nationalists had been trying to embarrass her by putting out false stories. When she died in 1981, the official Beijing obituary gave her birth date as January 27, 1893, and her age at death as eighty-seven—the Chinese consider a person a year old when he is born. I was amused to see that my original 1972 calculation had been correct.

An elderly woman's preoccupation with the facts or fictions of age and marriage in no manner detracted from the reality of Soong Chingling's life as a patriot of her country, a woman of daring, courage, and dedication, a great lady of the world. She had put her life on the line for China. She had never swerved from the principles of Dr. Sun Yatsen.

When, after Dr. Sun's death, she had been courted by General Chiang Kaishek (Sun's military commander), she firmly rebuffed him, perceiving in his courtship a desire to add the aura of China's heroic first president to his own political wagon. Ironically, Chiang turned to Chingling's younger sister, Meiling, who became his wife and political partner.

Chingling's ardent independence, her preference for China's Communist leaders who had worked closely with Dr. Sun Yatsen placed her life in danger. Nationalist assassination squads put on their hit list Chinese public figures who thought the Communists better allies in the struggle against Japan than Chiang Kaishek.

Chingling stood fast, but her brother, T. V. Soong, a righthand man of Chiang Kaishek in the convoluted world of Chinese politics, provided a round-the-clock security guard at her mansion on Rue Molière in the old French quarter of Shanghai. It was a reasonable precaution. At the same time it gave T. V. Soong a pretty good idea of the company Chingling was keeping.

Chingling made her mansion on the secluded street a safe house for Communist party agents on the run. She permitted the party (athough this was long denied) to establish in her attic a shortwave wireless facility that maintained contact with agents in the hinterland and even, it long was rumored, with Moscow. There was never a moment in the 1930s when

Madame Soong was not in physical peril. And there was never a moment when she gave thought to curtailing her activities because of that peril. The list of Communists whose lives she sheltered will never be known.

Chingling's life was endangered so often she could remember only the most perilous moments—1927, when Chiang Kaishek turned on the Communists and she made her way secretly out of China by Russian freighter to Vladivostok and by the Trans-Siberian Railroad to Moscow.

After a couple of years she returned to the Rue Molière house. It became the center of a web of conspiracies so intricate she could not remember all the details. Her house was watched not only by T. V. Soong's guards but by agents of the British, the Japanese, Chiang's secret police, the Americans, and the French.

The Rue Molière house was Chingling's beloved home for thirty years. In 1980 she was looking forward to retiring and going back. She scorned Henry Pu Yi's palace with its chinoiserie, decor of scrolls, heavy mahogony, and ebony furniture. She would point to the red-tasseled and gilt lights swinging from the ceiling and utter the words "Palace lights!" with loathing.

One thing Chingling made clear for years. She supported the Communist party but was not a member. She was an independent woman and an independent force. She never ceased to honor the memory of Dr. Sun Yatsen. She told Edgar Snow that the only Chinese politician she ever trusted was Dr. Sun Yatsen because "he had a world mind not a Chinese mind." Snow was shocked. "What about Mao?" he asked. "I distrust him less than the others," she replied. That was half-true. She respected Mao for his revolutionary achievements and his bringing unity and nationhood to China, but she did not like him personally—his peasant ways, his peasant manners, his barnyard vulgarity. Her favorite was

Zhou Enlai. They were kindred spirits, sophisticated, wise in the ways of China and Communist politics. Zhou was her confidante. She had little use for Zhou's wife, Deng Ying-chao, whom she thought dogmatic, dowdy, and dull. On the wall of her Pu Yi palace she put a photo of Zhou playing with her two young wards, Yolanda and Jeanette Sui. "He wanted children so much," she would sigh.

No moment in Chingling's life was more hazardous than her wartime escape from Hong Kong. She made her way there when the Japanese occupied Shanghai. She had simply turned over the Rue Molière house to two American women and walked out, a cheery fire burning in the fireplace, into a gray rainy day on the arm of the New Zealander Rewi Alley, who escorted her past the Japanese soldiers, chatting as if going for an afternoon stroll. He put her on a ship waiting in the Huangpo, and she was off to Hong Kong.

When Pearl Harbor day came, she got out of Hong Kong on the last plane for Chongqing, leaving the small Hong Kong airfield just ahead of the Japanese. Another New Zealander, the writer James Bertram, got her to the airport.

If Chingling felt any fear on these occasions, it was not visible.

The founding of the People's Republic brought Chingling a respite from physical danger—but not entirely. With the rise of the Cultural Revolution in 1966, she was again at risk.

Chingling had no use or respect for Mao's teenage Red Guards. Unlike some Chinese personalities, she did not don a red kerchief and, Little Red Book in hand, shout hosannas in Tiananmen Square to Chairman Mao. The Red Guards attacked her beloved Rue Molière house, threw furniture, books, and treasures into the street. They were looking for Soong Chingling (who was in Beijing), as she was told, in order to chop off her beautiful long straight black locks. "I'll chop off their hair!" she retorted grimly.

Zhou Enlai, recognizing that Chingling presented an attractive target to the Red Guards, dispatched a platoon of PLA soldiers with orders to protect her with their lives. The company was stationed in the adjoining compound, the whole quarter protected by high walls topped with concertina barbed wire. No effort to penetrate this stronghold was mounted by the guards.

Six years later Chingling still responded with anger at the thought of the Cultural Revolution. She apologized to her dinner guests for the lack of civility in her household. It was impossible, she said, to get good servants. All of hers had been shipped off to "May-Seventh cadre schools" so that their thinking could be revised. "The new chefs are ignorant of Chinese cuisine," she said. It was impossible to get a decent Chinese meal in Beijing. You had to go to Paris.

These were trivial concerns for a woman who had made her own special niche in the Chinese pantheon. Her American education—she had been sent to prep school in New Jersey and then to Wesleyan College in Macon, Georgia, by her Americanophile father—had left an indelible mark. Charlie Soong felt that no people were more like the Chinese than the Americans, especially southerners. She smoked Panda cigarettes because they were made with Virginia tobacco, the mildest and best tobacco of all. Her father had given her an American name, as well as a Chinese one. She was Rosamond. Every American correspondent who met her in wartime Chongqing fell in love with her.

She spent much time reading, always something American. She was delighted when I arranged to send her the Sunday edition of the *New York Times*—she read the *Times*'s magazine and book review sections. When her favorite, I. F. Stone, closed his *Weekly* and started writing for the *New York*

Review of Books, I sent her that. She named her wards Yolanda and Jeanette Sui in the tradition of the romantic novels with which she grew up. Americans, she explained, are "so open, so kind, so generous." The longer she lived, the more American she became, the more she dreamed of going back and visiting once again in Georgia. She got a print of *Gone with the Wind* and had it run night after night in the cosy upstairs drawing room of her palace, filled with cretonne, and wicker chairs and stacks of American books and magazines. It looked more like the porch of a postbellum Georgia mansion than a Manchu palace. She was fascinated to hear that Americans often took home the remains of overly large dinners in "doggy bags." The same custom, she remembered, had prevailed in Canton. She took to sending her guests home with bags of oranges and mandarins and grapes and apples from her over-flowing table.

Nothing in her last years so delighted her as an American wedding for her ward, Yolanda, who was marrying a Chinese film star named Kuan Qunhou. It was right out of Chingling's memory chest of her Macon days. Yolanda's beautiful white satin gown might have been worn by Scarlett O'Hara at Tara. There was American rock and roll resounding from tapes brought back from New York by Jeanette, a wedding cake designed by Jeanette with a little bride and groom atop; American young people including a grandson of Iphigene Sulzberger, the American grande dame, daughter of Adolph Ochs, founder of the *New York Times*.

I saw Chingling in those days, her eyes sparkling as though it was her own wedding day, beautiful, easy, radiant. She looked marvelous. She said to my wife and myself, "I wish you could come every year." Lots of talk about corn-bread, hominy grits, turnips greens, southern fried chicken, and she remembered sleigh-riding in New Jersey in the winter when she was going to prep school.

A year later she was dead of leukemia. Dramatic funeral scenes are no less common in China than in Victorian England. In fact, Soong Chingling had told with relish of what happened when Mao Zedong's body lay in state in September 1976 in the Great Hall of the People.

His widow, Jiang Qing, had brought a great wreath which (she said) she had made with her own hands. It bore the inscription "To My Teacher from His Pupil Jiang Qing."

The effrontery of Jiang's wording enraged Mao's cousin Wang Hairong (whose name had been left off the list of family survivors), and she flew at Jiang demanding by what right she had called herself Mao's pupil. In an instant the two were at each other in the presence of the assembled Mao hierarchy. Each reached for the other's hair. Jiang's came off in Wang's hands. It was a wig, revealing her as bald as an egg.

Chingling despised Mao's widow. She cackled with laughter as she described the scene.

In the case of Soong Chingling the government had taken charge of the deathbed in the closing days of the illness. It was determined to turn the event into a major political move in Chinese-Taiwan relations.

All—or almost all—of Chingling's relations, many of them resident in Taipei, were invited, especially her sister, Meiling, widow of Chiang Kaishek. So were Chingling's elderly stepchildren, the sons and daughters of Dr. Sun Yatsen, the grandchildren of Chiang Kaishek, Chiang Kaishek's son, the president of Taiwan, cousins from America, Hong Kong, around the world, many of whom had not been on speaking terms for years.

Not all came. Madame Chiang Kaishek wanted to trade her invitation for permission to bring back to the mainland the ashes of Chiang Kaishek and inter them with appropriate ceremony at Nanjing, which had been Chiang's capital. Beijing wanted Madame Chiang to come to Beijing for the funeral, but the price was too high. They turned her down on the urn. So she refused to come.

But most of Dr. Sun's surviving children, their wives, widows of nonsurvivors, grandchildren, and Soong cousins came. The Sui girls, the closest living persons to Chingling, were present but not recognized, present physically but, it was said, not publicly because of fear this might strengthen the legend that they were, in fact, Chingling's natural daughters, a fancy that a look at the calendar quickly dispelled. Chingling was in her late fifties and early sixties when the girls, daughters of her bodyguard-cum-secretary, were born. The girls, beautiful and forlorn, were permitted to see Chingling a few times as she lay dying—five minutes at a time. For the most part they were told to stay in the garden out of sight of the steady stream of prominent political pilgrims to the bedside.

There was, of course, a reason for this. Chingling in her long life, her support of the Communist regime, her holding of the official office of vice president, had resolutely refused to join the Communist party. She regarded herself, in a sense, as above the Communist party, as she was above the Nationalist party—the true heir of China's founding democrat, Dr. Sun Yatsen. It was, she had long held, incompatible with her position to become a Communist party member with all that it implied by way of ceremony and discipline and remain true to Dr. Sun. And, as she had often pointed out, it was totally at odds with protocol that she should become a Communist party member while her sister, Meiling, was the wife and then widow of the chief of the Nationalist party, Chiang Kaishek.

Her position, she felt, was one of dignity and principle. But this was not a dignity or a principle shared by the stage managers of her death, the Communist party. In her closing hours, the party inducted her into its ranks. The act occurred

May 15, 1981, a breathtaking ceremony that would have stirred the admiration of Cardinal Richelieu. Whether Soong Chingling was cognizant of her deathbed conversion or had already slipped into a final coma will be the subject of speculation for generations. The Sui girls, strolling in the sunshine of the lovely park, sitting sedately in the garden, were told by an old woman servitor what had happened. But they were enjoined to breathe not a word. The day after the deathbed conversion, so the party announced, Soong Chingling was unanimously elected honorary president of the Chinese People's Republic. Whether the great lady was informed of the honor is a mystery.

Death finally came to Chingling at 8:18 P.M. May 29, 1981. The invitations to the funeral ceremonies were ready and waiting. The mourning ceremonies and viewing of the body were held from May 31 to June 2 in the Great Hall of the People. Burial in the Soong tomb in Shanghai was carried out June 4.

But there was one final act. Chingling had accumulated a fortune. She had told the Sui girls of her intention to make them her heirs and shown them her will written in Chinese and English, then had locked it in the drawer of her dressing table. She had taken her wedding ring off her finger, the one Dr. Sun had given her in 1914, and given it to Jeanette. She had given the girls other keepsakes.

When Chingling died the government took the keys to the dressing table. The girls never saw the will again.

Not all the Soong relatives had assembled out of pure respect and family ritual. There were those, who as Mr. Micawber would have said, had their "expectations." Whatever those may have been, they were not to be fulfilled. Before the funeral a representative of the party called the relatives together and told them what had happened—or the official version of what had happened. Chingling had joined the party on her deathbed. By the rules of the party, her fortune and possessions became the property of the Communist party. Any rights or promises Soong Chingling had made earlier were automatically canceled. "You don't have to wait any longer," the party man said. Sad, angry, and contentious, the relatives dispersed. Yolanda and Jeanette followed suit.

So ended the life of a great and brave Chinese woman, a giant of the twentieth century.

13

Roger Wilkins and Patricia King

THE SUMMER OF 1991 in Washington was unusually long and hot, and the atmosphere in the city was not pleasant. In late June President Bush had nominated a rather obscure black judge to replace Thurgood Marshall, who had resigned from the Supreme Court of the United States.

Roger Wilkins and Patricia King were admirers of Marshall. They had reservations about the nominee, Clarence Thomas. The couple were lawyers, legal scholars, man and wife, professionals of high standing, intensely interested in the law, the courts, and the Thomas nomination. Roger and I had been very close from the time he joined the editorial board of the *New York Times* in the days when I was associate editor and editor of the Op-Ed page, and when he and Pat were married they became even closer to Charlotte and myself.

Roger was professor at George Mason University at Fairfax, Virginia, and he had spent the early part of the year

studying the influence of slaveholders on the American Con-
stitution and, in particular, the role in the debates of George
Mason, a very large slave owner, and a strong opponent of
"the peculiar institution." Patricia was a professor at George-
town University Law Center.

Roger's reservations about Thomas were immediate, intense, and articulate.

"That's my personality," Roger said. "Patricia is different. I was the first black person to oppose Thomas. I wrote a
piece for National Public Radio saying he wasn't qualified."

Patricia was more deliberate. She didn't think Roger
should say "off the top of your head" that a black candidate
wasn't qualified. She wanted to read the record; she wanted
to talk it out with Roger and others.

"It took her a while," Roger recalled. "But she decided
after all that Thomas was not qualified."

By this time Thomas was testifying before the senate
committee, telling the story of his life. A group of women
came to Patricia and asked if she would testify. Roger thought
she should. He knew that Patricia had been influenced by
what she regarded as Thomas's callous treatment of his sister
and that she found the story of his rise from poverty pathetic,
but she still wasn't sure if she should go public.

"You know I am a very private person," she told Roger.
"I don't do all these things in public the way you do—do you
really think I can do it?"

Roger was certain she could and should. They talked
over the points she would make, and she decided to go ahead.
It was a very serious decision. She had considered it carefully,
but once she decided she went forward with confidence,
testifying quietly, intensely, telling the country what a black
lawyer thought about a black candidate for the Supreme
Court, very sure of herself, very sure that she had come up
through the same process as had Thomas from a very poor

black family to the Washington scene, very certain that there was nothing exceptional in Thomas's background, of his talk with his grandfather, of what he had gone through. It was the story of a thousand blacks, 10,000 blacks, of whole generations.

Patricia's testimony was not drawn out. It was pointed, and her very appearance drew a deadly and intense contrast to Thomas's lachrymose tale. Patricia was that way, a woman of great care in making up her mind, but irresistible once she had come to a conclusion.

"We've all come up that way," she said. Patricia was an attractive, well-groomed woman, a woman of quality. As she spoke quietly, logically, no emotion, her sincerity swept the hearing room like a cool fresh breeze in a soggy Washington afternoon.

Never had Patricia King been in the national spotlight. She had no idea how people would react—would she be deluged with hate mail? What about the black community— would it accept a black woman's testimony? Patricia King got a lot of mail. Not one hate letter. Only one that took strong exception to her views.

Roger did not appear before the Senate committee. He had made his position clear in articles, TV talk shows, the range of public issue appearances that had been an integral part of his life since he left the Justice Department with the coming of Richard Nixon and, following in the footsteps of his father, had gone into journalism.

Few people in his profession possessed the grace and eloquence of his style. As Patricia said later: "When he wrote about a person I could see, literally see, the man or woman. They were real. They came alive."

He had made a spectacular entry into Washington journalism. His friend Tom Wicker, the *New York Times* columnist, invited him to a Gridiron banquet, the great Washington ceremonial at which pundits, their patrons, and publishers assemble annually to "roast" the president.

Roger looked about the hall filled with tuxedo-clad men and suddenly realized he was sitting in an all-male, all-white sea. He and the mayor of Washington were the only blacks in the room. It struck him like a thunderbolt, and at the invitation of Philip Geylin, then editor of the *Washington Post* editorial page, he wrote a piece that became the article-of-the-year in Washington. It propelled Roger onto the editorial board of the *Washington Post*.

Not long after that Patricia King met—or rather, didn't meet—Roger. She was lunching in a Washington restaurant, and Roger passed by, pausing to say hello to her escort.

"Who is that man?" she asked. Her companion told her. "I want to meet him," she said. Nothing happened except that she learned Roger had a longtime girlfriend. She started following his career. She knew when he left the *Washington Post* and went to the *New York Times*, and she knew his style so well that she could spot his editorials. She read every one. For a while he had a column in the *New York Times*. It jumped from page to page, never two days in the same place (one of the *Times* editors didn't like Roger—didn't like blacks, in general).

Roger came back to Washington in August, 1980, and Patricia began asking friends to introduce her. "This went on from August to December," she said. Nothing happened. Roger never called, but he kept hearing about her from friends. Finally, one of them urged him to give Patricia a call. "If she is so wonderful," Roger said, "how come she isn't married?" The friend told Roger to go to a pay phone, call her up, and find out. He did. He telephoned and said, "Why don't we get a bite to eat?"

Patricia was sick in bed. She invited Roger over, and they

talked all night. The date was December 10, 1980. Two months later they were married.

Where had Roger and Patricia come from? Roger in 1992 was pushing sixty. He had been born into the black ghetto of Kansas City, a very segregated city in 1932. His father and mother were graduates of the University of Minnesota. His father, a brother of Roy Wilkins, took over editorship of the black weekly, the *Kansas City Call*, when his brother went to New York to begin his long career with the National Association for the Advancement of Colored People. Roger went to a black school in Kansas City named for Crispus Attucks, a black hero of the revolutionary war. When Roger's father died, his mother moved to New York. She was a YMCA secretary, and they lived in north Harlem, near a cluster of Jewish emigrés from Hitler's Germany. One of the children was Max Frankel, later to become editor of the *New York Times*. Roger and Max did not then meet. Roger's world was black Harlem. He lived among blacks, went to a black school (there were Jewish teachers there), a black society, a black world.

Overnight it all changed. Roger's mother married again, a black physician, and they moved to Grand Rapids, Michigan, an all-white world, an all-white neighborhood, an all-white grade school, a white high school, and finally the integrated University of Michigan. Not easy. Roger went through ritual hazing by the all-white youngsters on his street. He was saved from the harassment by a white paper boy who became his friend and protector until the boy's father made him stop.

Roger was smart, outgoing, attractive, good in conversation. He got along with people, and he wound up president of the student council in his all-white high school.

Pat King, born in 1942, had an even deeper ghetto background, born in Norfolk, Virginia, brought up by her mother (her father, like Roger's, was a newspaperman on the

127

Norfolk black weekly), living in the all-black Liberty Housing Project, playing in the black playground, going to a black grade school, a black junior high, and the one black senior high.

Patricia was good at her lessons. She hoped to go to Howard, the black University in Washington. But a high school teacher broadened her horizon. He told her she had talent. She should aim higher. Pick a white college. Get a scholarship. She followed the advice and picked Wheaton College in Norton, Massachusetts, of which she had never heard. Patricia took her first plane ride, her first train ride, spent her first night in a hotel, and went on to all-white Wheaton in a town that boasted no black families. Patricia was one of four black girls in her class. No other blacks in the school.

It was a disaster. Too much. She couldn't handle it. "I almost floated out of school," she said. She was a lost girl. "But then I discovered I was tough," she said. She went back for the second year, no scholarship, working as a waitress to pay her way. Her uncle mortgaged his house to keep her in college. She was determined to make her way and succeeded. She graduated from Wheaton with honors, president of the school, the most distinguished woman in her class.

What then? Out of the blue the CIA tried to recruit her. "It was a terrific honor for a black person," she remembered. "There was hardly a black in the agency, and a black woman? None."

Patricia took it seriously. They would pay her way through an advanced degree—Ph.D., law, whatever. It was tempting. The CIA started her through the processing and gave her a lie detector test. They began asking questions about her father, who had abandoned her and her mother years earlier—wasn't he a member of the Communist party? What did she know about this?

Patricia knew nothing. She was so furious she almost walked out. She did not conceal her anger. She knew she had flunked. To her surprise, they told her she had passed. And offered her a position.

Patricia knew it was a terrific honor. She knew no black person would believe she had turned down the CIA. She went to her mother. "My mother is a terrific person. She said 'You have to do what you have to do.' " She told Patricia she could come home and stay with her.

Patricia turned her back on the CIA and went to Harvard Law, working summers for the State Department. It was a hard world, but Patricia had the confidence to deal with it. "I learned that I was a tough person," she said. "I learned how to do what I had to do, as my mother said."

By the time Patricia graduated from Harvard Law in 1969, Roger had already gone through the most dangerous days of his life. That was in 1967–68, the time of the assassinations of Bobby Kennedy and Martin Luther King, Jr. Roger was in the Department of Justice then, working for Nick Katzenbach, with John Dorr, Warren Christopher in the fire brigade, civil rights, out in the riot areas, trying to spot trouble before it erupted, trying to measure response when it did boil over.

The Detroit days were frozen in Roger's mind. Regular army troops had been sent in after a fenzy of riot and fire like South Central's in 1992 Los Angeles. Roger and a colleague were driving along the Detroit River boulevard. It was night and a curfew was in effect. A Michigan state police car screeched to a halt in front of them, and four officers stalked up to Roger's car. Two blacks against four whites. The state police were hysterical, screaming: "Get out of that car!" Roger thought it was the end. He was thirty-five. His father had died at thirty-five. This was it. This was the way he was going to go. He and his companion screamed "Department of

Justice. Department of Justice." Roger didn't dare reach in his pocket for his credentials. The police didn't seem to hear what he was saying. "I thought I was dead," Roger said. Finally one officer understood the shouts. Roger said: "Just reach in my pocket. Get my credentials." The man did and saw that what they had been shouting was true—Department of Justice. Instantly all was okay.

It was okay for that night. A couple of nights later the Justice team was cruising again, curfew still in force. They had a large car, six men crowded in. On the left side sat three blacks—a driver, Roger, another black behind him; on the right side John Dorr in front, Warren Christopher behind him, and a third white. If you approached the car from the left, it appeared all black. From the right it was all white.

Detroit was quieter. The shooting had died down, but the National Guard was still on duty. Guardsmen halted the car, approaching from the left, snapping: "What are you doing here?"

Roger called "Department of Justice" and started to reach in his pocket for his ID. Then he felt the steel of a gun barrel on his forehead and heard a voice saying, "If you move a muscle you are dead."

Roger froze. John Dorr reached over and displayed his Justice credentials. The moment passed.

Patricia did not go through the physical perils that Roger experienced. She was ten years younger, and when she took her turn working on civil rights for the government the hatred had softened a bit. And in Norfolk she had lived in a watertight black kingdom, no whites, few rough edges of black-white conflict. It was segregated but safe.

When Patricia entered the white world at Wheaton, the students and professors made her feel that she belonged. Not that there were no ethnic feelings, but they were directed against Jews, not blacks.

Perhaps it was because he had become a professor at George Mason University that Roger's attention became deeply engaged in an analysis of the origins of racial conflict in the United States and why the American dream had faltered. He found his answer in the dichotomy that had so long existed between noble words and reality, the reality of George Mason and his role as the antislavery slave owner. Few today remember that America in 1776 was a slave society and had been since the colonists first came.

The founders' guarantee of "life, liberty, and the pursuit of happiness" did not apply to "property," that is, blacks. It only applied to the actual electorate, possibly 150,000 white, male property holders. Only that minority was covered by the declaration that "all men are created equal." Not until Abraham Lincoln's Gettysburg proclamation November 19, 1863, would America be described as "dedicated to the proposition that all men were created equal" in a nation "conceived in liberty" with a "government of the people, by the people, and for the people."

By Lincoln's day America had existed as a slave nation for 245 years. Since then only 125 years have passed. No wonder the system and the prejudices of people are still skewed.

This reality did not temper the dedication of Roger Wilkins and Patricia King to the struggle for a more perfect society.

In the spring of 1992 they spoke together (but individually) at Wheaton College's commencement. Each took as a theme the events in Los Angeles South Central. On the platform with them was their nine-year-old daughter Elizabeth and Grayce King, Patricia's mother.

Each spoke of the family in America. Patricia took her mother as role model, a woman who raised by herself (her husband long gone) two girls, instilling in them the virtues of responsibility, sacrifice, and commitment. "We are," Patricia said, "paying a terrible price because of people who confuse freedom with irresponsibility or just plain selfishness. Responsibility, sacrifice, and commitment to family matters must be placed at the top of our personal agendas."

Roger probed deep into the economic and social wreckage underlying South Central, most of all an unemployment rate of forty-five percent among black males. "It has been that way for a long time," he said. "People disintegrate, people of all races, and do awful things to themselves and other people. Children are born and they are raised with chaos in their souls." He called on America to embark on "the most powerful family program I can possibly conceive—a massive two-track job program." Only jobs and jobs alone, he declared, could bring America, all of America, black, white, of all colors and creeds, back together and place the country on a foundation in which the old American dream might come true.

Neither Pat King nor Roger Wilkins spoke any easy words. There were none for the task they envisaged. They spoke tough common sense and would go on speaking tough common sense for the rest of their lives.

14

Andrei Dmitrievich Sakharov

LIKE MOST AMERICANS I knew nothing of the world of the Russian *intelligent* before I began my long years in Moscow as a correspondent of the *New York Times*.

The Russian *intelligent* is not the equivalent of a western intellectual. He may be a writer, an artist, an urban planner, a scientist, a bureaucrat, or a schoolteacher (as so often depicted in Chekhov's plays). Tolstoy was a member of the landed aristocracy and an *intelligent*. Dostoyevsky was an *intelligent* from the lower middle class. So was Vladimir Ulyanov, better known as Lenin.

An *intelligent* possessed a special way of thinking which arose in the nineteenth century, that of an educated individual who assumed an obligation to put his talents to the use of his country and his countrymen, a debt which he owed to the *narod*, the Russian people, and specifically to the *cherny narod*, the dark masses.

Andrei Dmitrievich Sakharov was born into the scientific

intelligentsia in 1921, and it is this circumstance that gave his life its selflessness and luminosity.

The *intelligent* had the moral imperative of speaking the truth as he believed it. Andrei Sakharov never lost this trait. It was in this spirit that Tolstoy wrote his memorials to the czar and Chekhov embarked on his long journey to Sakhalin to investigate the conditions of the exiles. And this inspired a generation of idealistic Russian youth to give their lives "going to the people" to try to bring them enlightenment. The Russian *intelligent* believed in the perfectibility of man and of his duty to put sacrifice above self.

Only by understanding this can you begin to know Andrei Sakharov. He is not to be explained as a man who dedicated his life to the special cause of world understanding or the elimination of Russian boorishness toward dissent. He possessed the *intelligent*'s dedication to the use of his abilities for the "good of the cause." He also was a genius.

I never managed to meet Andrei Sakharov face-to-face, although for a time I had more to do with the introduction and dissemination of his ideas to the western world than anyone else. It is a role of which I am proud. But we never managed to sit down in his cluttered apartment to share a glass of tea or to spend a long evening talking about Russia and the world. We tried, but the best we could manage was an occasional overseas telephone conversation and the exchange of letters.

Sakharov was born too late to experience the revolutions of 1917, but his family ardently supported the February revolution and an end to the oppression of the Romanov regime. The Sakharovs were a Moscow family, and they lived in one of the great apartment houses built in the early 1900s in what is roughly called the Arbat, a region now virtually obliterated by the Khrushchevian and Brezhnevian "improvements" but then a nest of solid mansions built by the old

Muscovite "White City" burghers and studded with well-appointed new buildings boasting apartments of ten or twelve or even fourteen rooms.

This was the milieu in which Sakharov grew up. His family was so vast, so many aunts, uncles, cousins, nieces, and nephews that it was able to preserve the whole of its flat even under the cramping of the Lenin-Stalin days when "communal apartments" became a euphemism for overcrowded slum.

Sakharov remembered a sunny childhood, a big closely knit family, dedicated to good works and intellectual curiosity. His father was widely known as a physics teacher and author of popular science works. He taught at the Moscow Pedagogical Institute. He played the piano for pleasure and during the civil war worked as a house pianist in silent movie theaters, providing accompaniments to the Mary Pickford and Douglas Fairbanks films and a little income in a Moscow that was even more disoriented than the Moscow of today.

Sakharov was educated at home by his father and his uncles. The family revolved around his grandmother until she died in the 1930s. He remembered that when he finally went to public school, he had difficulty in adjusting. He was so used to associating with adults, he had trouble relating to classmates of his own age.

Sakharov enrolled in the physics department of Moscow University at seventeen on the eve of World War II. When the Germans attacked June 22, 1941, he was not called to the colors. Talent like his was too precious. He was swiftly evacuated with a dozen others in his elite class to remote Ashkhabad on the Caspian Sea, far from the Nazi advance. But by the time he graduated in 1942, the most brilliant member of his class, the Germans had come within fifty miles. Sakharov was sent to a logging camp in the mountains, but only briefly. He had demonstrated his remarkable abilities and within weeks was co-opted to a military production unit where he perfected several new techniques. Here he wrote his first original works in physics and before war's end had been picked by Russia's Nobel-winning nuclear physicist Igor Tamm, who put him into his special unit at the Lebedev Physical Institute.

The nuclear arms race moved ahead. The Americans had exploded A-bombs in Japan in August, 1945. Alerted by their spies, the Russians were racing to catch up. Sakharov did not participate in making the atom bomb. That was in the hands of Secret Police Chief Lavrenti P. Beria and the KGB. In September, 1949, Beria turned out the first Soviet A-bomb ten years ahead of U.S. estimates.

The task of Sakharov and Tamm was to leapfrog the United States by producing a hydrogen bomb. They solved the H-bomb problem by 1950, and the first weapon was completed in 1951, ahead of the United States by several months. I was in Moscow at the time but knew nothing of these events.

This stunning achievement left no doubt of the genius of Sakharov. He was only thirty-one in 1951 and the most gifted physicist in the world. The Soviet Union showered him with every gift at its disposal—special privileges galore, a $30,000 yearly salary (twenty times the pay of an ordinary Soviet worker), luxurious living quarters, a car and chauffeur, an open option on any equipment, device, or facility needed for his research and—total anonymity. His name had already vanished from scientific journals, his contacts with the outside world severed. He began a life totally controlled by the KGB apparatus. His laboratory was moved to distant Turkestan. His friends did not know whether he was alive or dead. He become a bird in a very gilded cage.

Sakharov possessed one of the great brains of his time. He was a man who ranked with Rutherford, Einstein, Bohr,

Heisenberg, Kapitza, and Oppenheimer, men whose minds had changed the world. But Sakharov was a nonperson. As I well knew, censorship was total.

How did this scientific supernova respond to his role in creating the deadliest weapon man had known? At the simplest level, as he later said, he felt he was "working for peace." When he and Tamm began their collaboration, the United States possessed a commanding lead over Russia. It had monopoly of the A-bomb. Not until 1949 did the Soviet Union conduct its first A-bomb test. How close the United States was to an H-bomb or some even more exotic weapon Moscow could not judge. Sakharov told himself that his work was in the interest of human survival. If both the United States and the Soviet Union possessed nuclear capability, there would be a balance of terror which Sakharov was convinced would compel negotiations that would secure world peace.

"We were all convinced," Sakharov said, "of the vital importance of our work for establishing a worldwide military equilibrium, and we were attracted by its scope."

Sakharov's reasoning was not unlike that of many other great names in nuclear physics—Oppenheimer, Bethe, Szilard, and Kistiakowsky. They, too, convinced themselves that terrible as were the weapons, the end would be world peace. It may be significant that among them was one man who refused to join in nuclear weapons work. This was Peter Kapitza, who had been lured back to the Soviet Union in the 1930s from Rutherford's laboratory at Cambridge. Kapitza turned down Stalin's request to join in and was confined to house arrest for years.

Sakharov was still incredibly young, a slim, blond, diffident, scholarly man, totally caught up in physics. He later said he had done his best work at twenty-two. At thirty-two he was elected a full member of the Academy of Science. No one had ever been elected at such an age. Sakharov was convinced that the best work in physics and mathematics was done in the early years, and this conviction produced his first public intervention. He was barred from making public statements on science, but he could speak on education. In 1958 he and a colleague wrote a letter opposing a plan of Nikita Khrushchev's to compel students to break off their education at fifteen or sixteen and spend three years in "practical work" in factories and in the fields. Khrushchev was willing only to exempt very special cases like young girls in training to be ballerinas at the Bolshoi.

Sakharov denounced the scheme. He proposed instead that gifted students be pulled out of ordinary classes at the age of sixteen or seventeen and put into special intensive studies. He argued that the decade from sixteen to twenty-six was the most fruitful for intellectual achievement. He urged that mathematics instruction be revised to drop traditional Euclidian geometry, algebra, and trigonometry in favor of contemporary disciplines like probability theory, analytic geometry, and vector analysis.

Khrushchev backed down, and Sakharov won his battle—but it was almost his last victory. When he tried to use his influence to halt nuclear testing, he hit a stone wall. But this did not cause Sakharov to turn off his mind or his conscience as an *intelligent*. There is something in the makeup of great physicists that carries them beyond the formulas into the infinitely more complex and unpredictable phenomena of human society.

Sakharov followed the road set by Einstein and Oppenheimer but from behind a wall of security precautions which long kept him from the eyes of observers. Even with my preoccupation with Soviet affairs, until 1968 I had never heard his name.

Khrushchev was unremitting in his praise for Sakharov, but this was for his scientific achievements. He labeled him a naive politician, a man who did not understand power and the necessity of the Soviet Union to negotiate from a position of strength. Khrushchev's words could not stop Sakharov's mind. Step-by-step his concern with world questions grew. Each time he spoke out, more of his scientific freedoms were curtailed. He finally was demoted to work in the original Tamm laboratory where his meteoric career had begun. But as an *intelligent*, regardless of consequences, he could not hold his tongue. As he said: "I gradually began to understand the criminal nature not only of nuclear tests but of the enterprise as a whole. I began to look on it and other world problems from a broader, human perspective." When he found he could not curb the nuclear genie, he was seized with a terrible feeling of powerlessness. "I became a different man," he said. "I broke with my surroundings. It was a basic break."

All his life Andrei Sakharov was a gentle, retiring man, almost a romantic man, never losing the convictions of an *intelligent* which he had acquired in his family circle. His most characteristic expression was a kindly smile even in the most frustrating circumstances. He never sought special consideration for himself. In his last years he suffered from a heart condition, but there was never a complaint. He was self-assured in his special world of physics, but he spoke with a soft polite voice and presented his views with unfailing deference.

Because of his special status, his questions about nuclear weapons, weapons testing, nuclear policy, and the possibility of agreements with the United States came slowly, and when he did raise them he was told bluntly that these were none of his business. He was to attend to his bombs, and the government would attend to politics. It was a rude awakening for this quintessential *intelligent*.

He began to ask other questions. He pressed a serious indictment against the pseudo-scientific politician Trofim Lysenko, a Stalin favorite, whom Khrushchev had taken under his protection. Lysenko had destroyed Soviet genetics and biological sciences (and some of the scientists as well) and had threatened to do the same with mathematics and physics. Sakharov demanded an end to this. Khrushchev was furious. He threatened to have the KGB "teach this upstart a lesson" but fell from power before he could carry out his threat.

As time passed, Sakharov became aware that the evils he tilted against were not random and accidental but organic, stemming from the nature of the society created by Lenin and Stalin. The fault was not aberrational, mismanagement, individual criminality but the Communist system. He began to apply his intellectual powers to a study of the world in which he was living. His concerns that the limited liberalization of the Khrushchev period might come to an end in a resurgent Stalinist repression caused him in 1966 to join with twenty-four other *intelligenti* in a petition to the Twenty-third Congress of the Communist party, warning against the rise of neo-Stalinism and the danger of a rehabilitation of Stalin himself. Among those who stood with Sakharov were his fellow physicists Tamm and Kapitza, the novelist Konstantin Paustovsky, the ballerina Maya Plisetskaya, and the grand old man of Soviet diplomacy, Ivan Maisky, who for years had slept with a pistol under his pillow ready to take his life rather than submit to KGB arrest.

The impact on Sakharov's mind of the shoddy Soviet Union in which he lived in the mid-1960s produced his great work *Progress, Coexistence, and Intellectual Freedom*.

This treatise could not be published in Brezhnev's Russia. It circulated only in underground *samizdat*, that is, in clumsily duplicated sheets, passed from hand to hand. That is how I first learned of Sakharov. I managed to obtain a copy of his manifesto. It moved me deeply. Here from the depth of

Russia came a program for revival and renewal not only of Russia but of the world. I published it in the *New York Times* and then in a small book that was extraordinarily widely circulated. It was reprinted in almost every country of the world except China and Russia. The sensation was universal. Across the United States scientists and others formed Sakharov circles to discuss his ideas. Public forums were convened. Nothing that had come out of Russia since the time of Lenin attracted such attention. There was not a line in the Russian press about Sakharov, no acknowledgment of his existence, not even an attack on his ideas. In his native land Sakharov was still a nonperson. American universities and the universities of other nations showered down invitations. Sakharov was invited to deliver commencement lectures, to teach, to take up the chair of physics. The Soviet foreign office was buried in requests for permission for Sakharov to leave the country. The Kremlin did not move a muscle. Not one request received an answer.

In *Progress, Coexistence, and Intellectual Freedom* Sakharov called for the creation in Russia of an open society, free debate, free elections, political parties, democratic institutions, freedom of thought, freedom of expression, an end to Communist tyranny, abolition of censorship, a halt to human rights violations, the guarantee of a rule of law, a ban on political trials, political imprisonment, and forced labor. He asked that the process of de-Stalinization begun under Khrushchev be resumed and completed as a barrier to what he felt was a rising tide of neo-Stalinism. He did not call for an end to the Communist party (to which he himself had never belonged) but asked that it take the lead in the campaign to revive the nation.

His economic proposals called for full reform of the bureaucratic command system, which he characterized as obsolete and counterproductive. Russia was headed toward nemesis. In an addenda to his manifesto he spelled out his

economic ideas more fully. The Soviet system was incapable
of meeting the challenge of the computer era, which he called
the "second industrial revolution." The West was rapidly
computerizing industry, business, education, and government, producing thousands of uses for and varieties of computers. Children were trained to do their lessons on computer.
In Russia computers were regarded as a danger to the state.
They were under KGB control. Ordinary scientists, students,
and researchers had no access to the few machines that were
held under lock and key.

Sakharov proposed the freest possible interchange of
ideas and circulation of information. Without this, the Soviet
Union was doomed. Its creative resources were crippled.
Shackles must be removed from Russian minds.

"There is," he wrote, "no way out of the difficulties
facing the country except a course toward democratization
carried out by the party in accordance with a carefully worked
out program."

Sakharov asked for the end of the cold war. The United
States and the Soviet Union must pool their resources in an
attack on the world's social and economic ills: underdevelop-
ment, backward agriculture, unequal distribution of resources, ignorance, lack of capital resources, pollution of air,
water, and land, and environmental destruction.

Only joint action of Washington and Moscow could create
an atmosphere that would liberate the creative resources of
the superpowers and marshal them in an offensive against the
rapidly rising threats to the existence of the human race.

The program won Sakharov worldwide acclaim. At home
he faced intensified repression. He was deprived of possibilities for work as a physicist and subjected with his family to
continual harassment. His wife died, and when he married
Elena Bonner, half-Jewish, half-Armenian, daughter of a
woman who had spent sixteen years in Stalin's camps, active

in the dissident movement, the repressive campaign intensified.

Now Sakharov, strongly influenced by Bonner, began to shift from broad questions of the reorganization of the Soviet Union and convergence with the United States to a bitter struggle within the Soviet Union on behalf of human rights.

Sakharov was to be found in zero-degree weather demonstrating against the persecution of dissidents and taking his place in unheated courtrooms to witness the summary trials that condemned them to Arctic labor camps. He met with foreign correspondents to deliver copies of the protests that he directed almost daily to the government. He was using his world prestige on behalf of persecuted citizens whose names he hardly knew.

The life of the great humanist turned into a day-by-day struggle with KGB plainclothes agents. Any visitor who slipped through the twenty-four-hour guard at Sakharov's door was detained for questioning and sometimes prison. Telephone calls were monitored and often (as I came to know) interrupted. His mail was intercepted. All of this Sakharov endured with remarkable restraint. His wife boiled over in violent indignation.

Sakharov would accept no proposals from abroad to journey out of the land. As an *intelligent*, he felt that his place was in his own country. Russia, he believed, faced descent into chaos and the rank of a second-rate country. In 1975 he was awarded the Nobel prize for peace, but Brezhnev would not permit him to go to Oslo to receive it. Instead Sakharov was sent in 1980 into exile in the provincial city of Gorky, the former Nizhni-Novgorod on the Volga. All of his honors and prizes were declared invalid.

In Gorky, Sakharov lived a spartan life with his wife. He no longer could maintain contact with the outside. Only when his wife managed to travel to Moscow did the world learn what was happening to him. Once again he had become a nonperson. His neighbors did not know he was living next door. The country at large did not know if its most famous citizen was alive or dead.

Not until Mikhail Gorbachev came to power was Sakharov permitted to leave his exile, brought back to Moscow, elected to the Soviet parliament, and hailed by Gorbachev and the country as Russia's true prophet, its moral conscience. He was recognized as the man who a quarter century before, in 1968, had glimpsed the future, had forecast the inevitable descent of Russia into the abyss, who had proclaimed that its salvation must be abandonment of its command economy, the Communist party monopoly of thought, and the introduction of a new free and democratic society. For those words Sakharov had been called a political naive whose *Progress, Coexistence, and Intellectual Freedom* had stitched together "a conglomeration of ideas from the Gospel, Rousseau's social contract, and the American Bill of Rights."

Sakharov had then responded that he was not a professional politician and that this was perhaps why he continued to be bothered by questions of a moral nature.

"I shall refrain from specific predictions," he said not long before he was recalled to Moscow, "but today as always I believe in the power of reason and the human spirit."

Sakharov's confidence was not misplaced. When he died in 1989 all Russia and all the world mourned. Russia had not reached the levels to which he had aspired. Perhaps it never would. But the Russia that was being created in the image of his ideas was struggling valiantly to work its way out of the miasma.

If I had nothing else as a legacy of my Russian years, the minor role I played in spreading the ideas of the supreme *intelligent*, Sakharov, would shine in my mind like a medal. Seldom in a busy life does one have the opportunity to play handmaiden to ideas that have changed the world.

15

Black and White in Birmingham

On the morning of April 6, 1960, I checked into Room 1117 of the old Tutwiller Hotel in Birmingham, Alabama. I had been traveling almost continuously, reporting on the new civil rights movement, and now I had gotten to Birmingham, which many had called the Gibraltar of Segregation in America. The rest of the world might change. Not Birmingham.

Birmingham was not, I had been warned, a safe place for reporters, and I was nervous and a bit on guard. The bellhop put my bag down in Room 1117 about 9:30 A.M. I still had not unpacked when the desk clerk called and said they'd made a mistake. They were switching me to Room 1060.

Not until 1956 did I learn why my room had been changed. By carelessness I had been booked into a room that had not been bugged. On orders of the Birmingham police, any newsman or person suspected of being in the civil rights movement was given a room wired into the police taping system set up by Theophilous Eugene Connor, commissioner of police. Connor, a onetime radio talk show host, possessed a mellifluous voice. He listed himself in the telephone directory as Bull Connor, and he was a man of strong opinions ("Segregation yesterday, segregation today, segregation forever"; "Damn the law: in Birmingham I am the law").

Passions ran high in the Birmingham of 1960, and real danger lurked barely under the surface. It was clear and present. Over a dispatch that I wrote, the *New York Times* placed the headline: "Fear and Hatred Grip Birmingham."

My story said: "From Red Mountain where a cast-iron Vulcan looks down 500 feet to the sprawling city, Birmingham seems veiled in the poisonous fumes of distant battle. . . . More than a few citizens, both white and Negro, harbor growing fear that the hour will strike when the smoke of civil strife will mingle with that of the hearths and forges."

The city fathers erupted in anger at my image of their metropolis and proceeded to file millions of dollars in libel suits against me and the *New York Times*. A warrant was sworn out for my arrest should I ever set foot again on the soil of fair Alabama.

Just a year later, May 14, 1961, the deadly violence that I had predicted burst out. Mobs armed with iron pipes and blackjacks stormed the Birmingham bus depot and attacked a group of freedom riders. Wounded men and women were beaten to the pavement. Blood flowed across the creosote.

The *Birmingham Daily News*, which had exploded in rage at my dispatch, now wrote that on Mother's Day "fear and hatred" had indeed overcome Birmingham as I had predicted. Nor was that all. Still ahead lay the attack by police dogs and club-wielding deputies on the Reverend Martin Luther King, Jr., and his followers, King's letter from the Birmingham Jail and the dynamite blast that killed four little black girls attending Sunday school at the Sixteenth Street Baptist

Church. Soon the name Birmingham became a synonym for violence and oppression.

I met some remarkable people in Birmingham, none more so than Cecil Roberts and Bessie Estell. For thirty or forty years Cecil Roberts made things happen in Birmingham. By the time of her death in 1991, Birmingham had become a monument to change in the rock-bound racist South. And Bessie Estell's vaulting career had become a symbol of black partnership in the new Birmingham.

Cecil Roberts used to say: "I never went to college. My college was the *New York Times*." There was a bit of truth to this. But only a bit. What was true was that in her forty years of public life the *New York Times* had become in her hands an instrument of her ceaseless crusade for a better life for the people of Birmingham, black and white.

Cecil was born in England. On the eve of World War I her parents took their large family (Cecil had six brothers and four sisters) to the south of France. When war came one brother wheeled Cecil to the railroad station in her baby carriage. It was a narrow escape, but Cecil's life would be filled with alarums and triumphs against the odds.

All her life Cecil preserved a light but unmistakable English accent. She was at some pains to retain it, and when she came to Birmingham it instantly set her apart in that land of Tom Heflin drawl. But she was not really English. Her father was a midwestern American named Edward Johnson who had moved to England, where he met Cecil's mother. They had a house in Surrey until Cecil was eight years old. "My father," she once told me, "inherited wall-to-wall mortgages." After World War I they wound up in Long Island "in the potato country playing around with horses." At seventeen she was working at Bonwit Teller, first as a salesgirl, then as a model and fashion consultant. She loved it.

She met David Roberts, III, son of Birmingham's first

family, toward the end of World War II. She was engaged at the time, but David swept her off her feet. She had never met anyone so honest, so good, with so much integrity. They met on December 18, 1943, and eloped and were married February 12, 1944. David was a naval lieutenant assigned to the battleship *South Dakota*. When David was released from the service in 1945, they went straight to Birmingham.

"She turned Birmingham upside down," David remembered nearly fifty years later. This was no exaggeration. The gritty, grim steel-and-coal town had seen nothing like Cecil. Her eyes sparkled, her grin was irrepressible, and she wore her chestnut hair like a crown. Her ruddy skin glowed with energy. Give her a Spanish shawl, and she could pose as a gypsy.

At first her talents turned to the arts, and long before her death she had become the first lady of music and theater in Alabama. She raised money for polio and the March of Dimes, Planned Parenthood, and welfare groups but quickly burst those bonds and was revitalizing and setting up theater groups. As a newspaper editor recalled: "She pressured us all to use our possibilities."

From the beginning Cecil couldn't stand the racial inequality. People called her a radical. "I wasn't a radical," she said. "I just wanted blacks to have the rights they paid for with their taxes. I didn't think everyone should integrate. I just thought we couldn't afford to maintain two systems."

Cecil Roberts set about to change the rules. She had no sympathy for words like "segregation" and "integration," and she let everyone know it. David stood by her. He was the third generation of a clan that had made a fortune in coal. Without David she could not have changed this Gibraltar of race, the city where the police commissioner swore he would not permit "blacks and whites to integrate together."

Cecil had flair. After she had raised enough money to

put Birmingham's Symphony Orchestra on its feet, she realized that it was not integrated. It played to an all-white audience. She changed that. Opening night in formal dress she walked down the center aisle, holding the arm of Birmingham's leading black businessman, and took her place with him in the first row, center aisle. Birmingham gasped but took the point.

The hate mail, the threats, the hints of retaliation became an everyday fact of life to Cecil. Sometimes she told the police; more often she didn't bother. She was fearless in her own person, driving her car alone into all-black neighborhoods, crossing every segregated pattern, heedless of the fact that Birmingham possessed a deadly dynamite-wielding Ku Klux Klan which had bombed churchs, schools, and the homes of civil rights advocates.

Cecil's telephone line was tapped, her mail was opened, and she was under almost constant surveillance by uniformed or undercover police. She paid no heed to this. Her relations with Bull Connor, whose nightstick-ready officers reinforced segregation with brutality, were equivocal. She often bantered with him and once told me that "I think he has a sneaking admiration for me."

I think Bull was afraid of Cecil. He assured her that he had her followed for her own protection, and this may have been at least partially true. Had anything happened to Birmingham's first citizen, he would have paid a heavy price. He could not cope with Cecil's irrepressible sense of fun. She got a supply of police nightsticks somewhere and put labels on them "Bull Connor Nightstick Award," sending them as Christmas presents to some national correspondents who had been in Birmingham. During the Little Rock school integration fight an editor called her for help in persuading a fiery black orator to postpone a speaking engagement to a less-troubled moment. Cecil pondered the problem, then said:

149

"Perhaps I can get Bull Connor to put him in jail." It was a joke—but just barely.

"Ol' Bull," Cecil once said, "could have arrested me many times for doing decent human things like taking blacks to places where it was against the law. Of course he knew what I was doing but he never arrested me."

In 1955 Birmingham voted Cecil Roberts their Woman of the Year. Not everyone agreed with her, but they had learned to respect her.

Twenty years later, in 1975, Bessie Estell was elected Birmingham's Woman of the Year. She was almost everything Cecil was not—quiet, careful, cautious, low profile, but superb in her profession, which was teaching—and black.

The selection in each case was made by the Junior Chamber of Commerce. Bessie Estell was bowled over. "I remember what I said when I heard the news: 'Birmingham has come a long ways.' "

Cecil Roberts had helped to bring the city along. So had Bessie Estell. She had spent her life in education, which she believed must be the cornerstone of the rise of blacks to equal status with whites. Integration served no real purpose unless it meant equal opportunity under the rules, a level playing field. And for that to come about, blacks must be educated and possess the skills they needed to take their place in a black-and-white society.

When I met Bessie Estell she had just been elected to the Birmingham City Council, the first black woman to hold such a post. She joined two other blacks on the council, a certain sign of their rise to a share of political power in a state where most adult blacks could remember not even possessing the right to vote.

Bessie Estell was a trim, handsome woman, perfectly groomed with a quiet but commanding presence. No one could speak with her without knowing that they were confronted with a woman of character, dignity, and knowledge. She spoke with precision, choosing her words carefully with only a light southern accent. She was in her fifties when we met, born in Alabama, a product of the black educational system, segregated schools, and the Tuskegee Institute. She had taught in Birmingham's segregated schools during her professional career, rising to head the number one black high school, which, in the opinion of educators, was not only the leading black school in the city but the best school in Alabama, black or white.

This was the quality of education that Bessie Estell believed would equip the blacks to compete in the new world that she saw opening up. She did not expect miracles. In the twenty years before we met she had brought the adolescents in her school through a period of deep traumas stemming from the seemingly endless violence in Birmingham, the bombings, the assaults, the relentless hatreds.

Bessie Estell had persisted. The worst thing had been the bombing that killed the four black Sunday school children. The worst thing, she thought, was that no one had then been arrested for the crime, although everyone whispered that the perpetrators were known.

But Bessie Estell believed the shock of that bombing had awakened Birmingham, much as Pearl Harbor had awakened America. It had convinced the people that action had to be taken. She had moved out of her chosen field of education to become a player in the new power group that was running Birmingham and heading it into the twentieth century.

She had become one of a small group of political and business leaders who met informally for breakfast every Monday morning with the mission of resolving problems before they boiled over. And, she believed, it was working.

Not long before we talked, she, herself, had organized and overseen arrangements for the largest meeting ever held in Birmingham, a black conference of the Baptist Sunday School Training Conference, 16,000 blacks pouring into the once iron-clad segregationist city, filling every hotel and motel for miles around, eating with the whites in every Birmingham restaurant, shopping and visiting in every Birmingham facility. There was not a single racial incident. That, said Bessie Estell, is evidence of a changed city.

"We still have not arrived," she said. "We have a lot to do before we sleep." She, as expected, put her first priority on education. Its quality for both blacks and whites had to be improved. And crime must be brought under control. That was an economic problem. As the economy of the working class improved, crime would automatically be reduced. There had to be better employment for black males and better income for all. So much crime and so much hatred were generated in the fierce competition of the underclass for jobs and wages.

One thing, she thought, would help Birmingham and Alabama—more conventions, more people coming in from the outside. It would help to shake things up. And bring in more income.

Like her friend Cecil Roberts, Bessie Estell was undaunted by every single obstacle she faced in life. She had overcome much. And she would go on fighting for more to the end of her days. She did not possess Cecil's flamboyance. But her work was equally effective, and she possessed equal courage.

Both women died in 1991, a grevious loss for the city they so loved and changed. Bessie Estell died quietly and conventionally. Not Cecil Roberts.

Cecil left special instructions for her burial. She was to be garbed in her favorite red silk dress. She was to wear the special "Yellow Dog Democrat" button she had devised ("I'll vote for a Yellow Dog if it's on the Democratic ticket"), and in her lap rested her reading glasses and a copy of the *New York Times*.

Once a friend had asked her what was her idea of Heaven. She said daily home delivery of the *New York Times*. What was her idea of Hell? To be without my reading glasses. Whatever her destination, Cecil Roberts was properly equipped.

16

Edgar Snow

NO REPORTER SO CAPTURED the imagination of his fellow newsmen in the years running up to World War II as did Edgar Snow of Kansas City, whose *Red Star Over China* was to become a classic.

Snow was twenty-two years old when he stepped ashore at Shanghai July 6, 1928. He had made some money in Wall Street, posed for Arrow Collar ads, played drums and saxophone in the Blue Bell Jazz band at the University of Missouri, and stowed away on a Japanese liner across the Pacific.

The most important item on that listing is "University of Missouri." It was Dean Walter Williams of the Missouri School of Journalism who set Snow off and running in China.

A romantic disposition took Snow across the broad Pacific. He fancied himself with his good looks, curly auburn hair, five-foot, nine-inch build, deep brown eyes, easy smile, warm and serious manner that appealed to men and women alike, a successor to Richard Halliburton, whose devil-may-

154

care books of personal adventure (swimming the Hellispont) delighted a generation of matrons of the 1920s.

In real life Snow was no Halliburton, but like many of his college mates he was smitten with wanderlust. He had already "ridden the rods" from Kansas City to the Pacific before he decided to cross it. China was the first stop in a plan to go around the world.

He never made it around the world. A letter from Dean Williams got him a job on the *China Weekly Review* in Shanghai, and he was hooked forever.

Snow arrived in China a carefree college boy. He matured quickly. His first big experience was a trip northwest into the great famine area around Saratsi, south of the Gobi. Hunger took six or seven million lives. Only Snow reported it first-hand—a small child covered with dust, sitting stunned beside an old man, already dead; withered women digging in dry earth for roots; bloated faces, bloated bellies, trees stripped of bark as high as a man could reach (food for the starving).

In the *New York Times* the famine warranted only a few paragraphs, but the image of the dead and the dying stayed with Snow as long as he lived and another image as well—the spectacle of Chinese walking past the victims in Saratsi with blank faces.

Snow was a supporter of Chiang Kaishek, but Saratsi convinced him that China needed "a crusader, a practical idealist" to lead it out of the "stench and decay."

Snow quickly became a professional. He filed for the *London Daily Herald*, the *New York Herald Tribune*, the *Saturday Evening Post*. He began to write books about his China experiences and he married Helen Foster, a beautiful American girl who landed in Shanghai in 1931 and herself became an ambitious reporter. The couple knew everyone worth knowing in the China of the 1930s. One of Snow's close friends was Madame Soong Chingling, widow of China's first president, Sun Yatsen.

Snow and his new wife moved from Shanghai to Peking. There at the American Yenching University they came to know many student activists, some with secret Communist links.

China was in turmoil, the Japanese menacing from the north, Chiang Kaishek indecisive, warlords forming power combinations, foreigners indifferent, and in the distant hills, it was rumored, a nascent Communist movement. The peasants thought it was led by a man named Zhu Mao, actually Mao Zedong and Zhu De.

No one had seen this Communist band. Its existence was denied by Chiang Kaishek; just some bandits calling themselves Communists, he claimed.

There was endless discussion in Shanghai, Canton, Peking, and Tientsin about the "Communist bandits." Periodically the Nationalists announced they had wiped them out. In a month or two there were more "annihilation" battles.

Snow decided to find out what was going on. He got a $750 advance in 1934 from his publisher for a book on "Red China or another topic." Whether he could get to "Red China" was dubious. Chiang Kaishek had set up a military blockade.

In fact, although neither Snow nor any correspondent knew it, Mao Zedong was moving his base away from Jiangxi Province in the south where Nationalist troops had surrounded him. He had embarked on a 6,500-mile trek through remote and difficult mountains and deserts and arrived in northern Shaanxi Province by late 1935 and early 1936.

Snow got Madame Soong to send word to the Communists that he wanted to visit them. Nothing happened. He tried every contact he could think of. Still nothing happened. After more than two years in this effort he got a nibble followed by a letter in invisible ink introducing him to Mao

Zedong. For years Snow was not certain where the letter came from or how he came to get it. Actually Snow's laissez-passez was the product of his perseverence, diligence, good timing, and—good luck.

Mao had been cut off not only from Shanghai and Peking but also from Moscow. His radio wasn't powerful enough to pick up Soviet signals or transmit that far. Now in northern Shaanxi contact was restored. An envoy reached Mao with urgent advice from Moscow: End your isolation. Let the world know about Communist China.

Mao followed this advice. Snow had been sending him message after message, so he got the call. Years later Snow discovered that Liu Shaoqi, the future president of China, had been sent to north China as Mao's secret representative. He employed some of the Yenching students who knew the Snows to pass on the letter in invisible ink. Snow was to go to Xian in northwest China and check in at a hostel. Someone would meet him there and escort him to Mao.

Snow slipped out of Peking on a slow Chinese train. Before leaving, he posted a letter to his publisher saying: "If I get through it will be a world scoop."

He did get through and it was a world scoop. *Red Star Over China* changed the world. Snow had made his way to Baoban, where he interviewed Mao Zedong. Mao told him the story of his life. Snow talked with Zhou Enlai; he met Zhu De; he had interviews with all the Communist leaders. He inspected the communes, the social programs, their rural work. He reported they were alive. They were real. They were Communists, not bandits, not a figment of Chiang Kaishek's paranoia. They were a political force, and in fifteen years they would win China. It was one of the great journalistic breakthroughs of the twentieth century. Snow got it through imagination, grit, skill, stubbornness, and bravery. There had been moments when he could easily have lost his life. He did not. He spent four months in the Communist area and came back with every important ingredient in the story. Even so, he almost lost his story—literally. A Red Army soldier mistakenly tossed Snow's bag with his notes and photos off the truck at a remote post. When Snow got to Xian, he found the bag missing. He spent a frantic twenty-four hours until it was safely retrieved and brought to him.

Snow's account changed China—a Chinese translation of *Red Star* was put into print before the American and English publishers got around to it. From that moment in 1938 *Red Star* has never been out of print. Every American going to China has read it. It was still the best guide to Red China more than fifty years after publication.

No work so influenced the prewar (and postwar) generation of American correspondents. I can remember the breathless awe with which I read it page-by-page, gobbling the 592 pages in two sleepless nights of excitement. Nothing gave me such realization of the power and scope of the world of reporting.

I had cut my teeth on Lincoln Steffens's autobiography, the classic account of the muckrakers of the early years of the American century, the men and women who turned their eyes and minds to the Shame of the Cities, as Steffens called it, the corrupt municipalities, and to the exposés of Chicago's "hog butchers," the evils of the great oil companies, of corporate greed in the 1900s. None of that packed the drive of Snow's clean, comprehensive account of this new society arising in the world's most ancient state.

I had, of course, devoured John Reed's remarkable account of the Russian Revolution, *Ten Days That Shook the World*. Like Snow, Reed had been an American newspaperman. Just out of Harvard, he was drawn by the excitement of the fall of Czar Nicholas II. He was on the scene when Lenin and the

Bolsheviks seized Petrograd. Reed wrote the only eyewitness hour-by-hour, day-by-day account. It became a classic.

Reed, like Snow, had positioned himself on the scene in Petrograd. He had run all over town, from Winter Palace to Smolny, from Nevsky Prospekt to Admiralty Square. He had talked to Lenin, had met Trotsky, had squirmed his way into the First Soviet session and listened as Lenin declared, "We will now proceed to construct the Soviet order."

There was, I think, a dynamic behind the classic works of Reed and Snow—why had it been American newspapermen who bore witness to the Russian and Chinese revolutions?

I did not believe it was accidental. No German, French, or English journalist could have matched the feat of the Americans. American newsmen are always on the scene of great events. They possess the energy, the creativity, the determination that propels them into the inner rooms of the Winter Palace or into Mao's cave to listen night after night as he tells how he came to lead the Chinese Revolution.

They do not necessarily get all of the story. But they get the gist. Certainly Snow could not get Mao to reveal the negatives, to detail the bloodiness of the Long March, the slaughter of the landlords, the infighting with his Russian peers. But those are details. Snow penetrated to the sanctum of the Communists, and he brought out the story of a movement that was going to dominate China and change the balance of power in the world.

It was this earnest, hardworking, persistent questioner with his warmth and his instinct for the right inquiry who put that story together; who took advantage of an opportunity that he had made for himself, to bring to the world one of the most important of emerging developments.

There were those after the fact who criticized Snow for not getting every point straight. That is trivial. He got the big points right and cleared the way for those who came after him to put in the footnotes.

Snow spent the rest of his life with China—although not always physically there.

During the McCarthyite period—and even before— Snow endured a firestorm of vapid but dangerous criticism. Like the old China hands of the State Department, he was vilified as a Communist dupe (in fact, often libelously described as a Communist) and charged with being one of those "who lost China."

In the atmosphere of hysteria, nothing Snow said could stem the vituperation. No matter what the outcry, Snow did not apologize. He said he was not a Communist nor a "Commysymp." He was a reporter who had gone to Red China's base and reported the facts as he had seen and understood them. He was not a partisan or a propagandist. Snow's response went unheeded in the McCarthyte witch-hunt. But it cost Snow his prized editorial connection with the *Saturday Evening Post* and ultimately, finding the atmosphere in the United States so poisonous, he moved to Switzerland and remained there the rest of his life.

He never spoke publicly of a greater irony. He was for practical purposes barred from Communist China in the very years of the slanderous attacks in the United States.

The inner mystery of Snow's relations with China and the Communists from the late 1930s to 1960 has not been unraveled. But despite the stunning popular success of *Red Star* in China, it touched off bitter undercover wrangling among Communist ideologues. One, a man named Hans Shippe, a German, appeared on the Snows' doorstep and tried to get Snow to withdraw his book. Ed refused. Shippe took his case to Mao Zedong, who shut up Shippe in anger and turned his back on him. Shippe left and ultimately was killed with the Fourth Route Army in a battle against the Japanese.

Snow spent the war years—and after—out of China. He went to Russia, to western Europe, to America, and ultimately to India where he witnessed Gandhi's assassination. But he did not return to China until 1960. When he got there Mao noted that he had not seen Snow for twenty-one years and said he had heard Snow had turned against his old Chinese friends.

Snow was shocked. He had been trying to get back to China since 1946, but none of his communications reached Mao. Getting no reply, Snow turned to his old friends, Rewi Alley, the New Zealander, and George Hatem, the Lebanese-American, both long resident in Beijing. He did not know that both of them had also been cut off from top-level access. Mao in 1960 did not seem to know that the two were still in China.

The evidence behind Snow's exclusion from China is hard to come by—a few cryptic remarks by Hatem and Alley, references in Snow's letters and journals. But some surviving Beijing hands are confident that in the paranoic party politics of the late 1940s and 1950s, Snow—and his friends—were targeted as "western spies" by Kang Sheng, China's "Beria." Xenophobia was rampant, and Snow had become a secret target, long before he was to be excoriated and *Red Star* denounced during the madness of the Cultural Revolution of 1966–67 and the years following. Snow remained tight-lipped about all this, but when it was over some of his Chinese friends let drop a few hints at the reality behind the Chinese facade.

Snow lay dying of cancer in Switzerland as Richard Nixon, after an exchange of letters with Snow, prepared for his epochal meeting with Mao Zedong in February, 1972, in Beijing. Snow did not live to see that day despite the gracious act of Zhou Enlai, who sent China's best physicians to Switzerland to try to prolong Snow's life. Two of Snow's close friends, George Hatem, who had made the trip to northern Shaanxi and who had stayed behind to become a surgeon with the Chinese Red Army, and Huang Hua, the Chinese student from Beijing who had acted as interpreter for Snow during his long talks with Mao Zedong, also went to Snow's bedside.

Snow died as Nixon's plane from Washington was approaching Chinese airspace. It had been upon a carefully composed Chinese hint to Snow in 1970 that Nixon and Kissinger had calibrated their overture for the Chinese-American rapprochment, a tangible monument to the reputation of Nixon whom Snow had despised since the early days of his political career as a dedicated anti-Communist.

With death, Snow entered the pantheon of American journalism. But, as if to demonstrate the hardihood of Chinese Communist politics, a few years later a monument was raised in China—not to Snow—but to Hans Shippe, the man who had exerted so much energy in campaigning against *Red Star Over China*. And some of Shippe's advocates hailed his contribution to the Chinese Revolution as greater than that of Snow.

17

Liu Binyan

A MAN ONCE TOLD LIU BINYAN that as he was reading one of his articles a surge of emotion passed through his body, a surge so powerful that his fingers tightened and crushed a glass he was holding. But, said the man, he felt no pain when the splinters pierced his hand and drew blood. Instead, he felt only euphoria from Liu's words.

That was the reaction of one of the tens of millions of Chinese who read *People or Monsters*, Liu Binyan's depiction of the debasement of life in China under Communist rule.

This was Liu's first article to appear after he had been freed January 24, 1979, from twenty-two years of imprisonment, exile, physical and spiritual torment. Mao himself had decreed Liu's arrest, commenting that "this man is interested in stirring up confusion." The "confusion" arose from Liu's powerful reportage of the society Mao had brought into being.

Liu was silenced on July 8, 1957. China passed through waves of change—Mao's chaotic Cultural Revolution, the deaths of two of his chosen successors, Liu Shaoqi and Lin Biao, and finally in 1976 the deaths of Zhou Enlai and of Mao himself. With the assumption of power by Deng Xiaoping, Liu Binyan's long travail, his harassing imprisonment, his struggle to survive in the frigid wastes of China's Mongolian frontier came to an end.

Hardly had Liu Binyan drawn his first free breath than he went back to his chosen task—the exposure of evil, the depiction of the ugly face of China's "dictatorship of the proletariat," and the banality of life under communism.

That China's dictatorship should have produced so courageous a journalist, the finest of our times, seems an irony of classic proportions. Is it not we Americans with our First Amendment privileges, our free and competitive press, our unfettered investigative reporting, our Woodwards and Bernsteins, our Sy Hershes, who lead the world in exposing the corruption of the high and mighty?

How could a man nourished in Marxist society, a devout, dedicated Communist party activist, publish reportage that shook his country to the core?

Anomaly it may be. Truth it certainly is. Many Chinese came to regard Liu Binyan as a force more powerful than that of his government—a fact that finally compelled him to leave his country because his life was in peril and his voice had again been strangled by censors and policemen.

I have known Liu Binyan for many years. He does not convey the image of a Savonarola. He was a quiet, sometimes diffident man of sixty-seven in 1992, clear-eyed, muscular. To Americans, there is something vaguely familiar about his appearance. He does not look quite Chinese. In fact, there is a hint of Mohawk or Iroquois in his aquiline nose, his proud head, his not-so-dark eyes with their flecks of gold. All of this, perhaps, is a heritage from his Manchu grandmother. He is not pure Han.

Liu Binyan grew up in Manchuria, China's vigorous industrial north country, born in Harbin, a city of mixed Chinese and Russian culture, almost a Russian city in the late days of the Romanov empire. His father was completely bilingual. Returning to China from Siberia in 1917, he was mistaken by the border guards for a Russian because of the perfection of his speech and his non-Han appearance.

It may be, as Liu Binyan sometimes thinks, that the international atmosphere of Harbin gave him a character more idiosyncratic than that of many of his countrymen. Han culture is closely integrated; deviance and dissent are discouraged; filial and clan loyalty combine to create uniformity of conduct and a surface submissiveness.

There is little of this in Liu Binyan. He is a man of free mind. He makes his own judgments, and he is remorseless in his quest for the facts, for the truth. His motto is identical with that of Deng Xiaoping: *Shi shi qiu shi*—seek truth from facts. Deng took it from Mao, who adapted it from the German of Karl Marx. None of the three realized that the first to use the phrase was Confucius.

Seek Truth from Facts. This became the essence of Liu Binyan's life—not the Truth of Mao, Marx, Deng, or Confucius, but Truth as Liu Binyan defined it. "I am not much of a Confucian," he explained. In his relentless search for knowledge and truth he was impelled by an irresistible inner urge. He could no more quell it than he could halt his heart from beating. And once he believed he possessed the truth, he could not lock it into his bosom. He was compelled to declare it—on the printed page or when he addressed a meeting. Again and again he told himself that he must be tactful and cautious, but when he stood on the platform his conscience would not let him speak a half-truth. Nor could he leave out that portion of a story which he knew would get him into trouble.

Liu Binyan had not expected to become a journalist or a man whose reportage would sway his country. He started out as a teenage revolutionary in the years when China was finding its way out of warlordism, World War II, Japanese aggression, and the struggle between Chiang Kaishek and the Communists for control of the future. Like many of his fellow high school students, Liu abandoned his studies for revolutionary activities—arranging parades, demonstrations, and meetings, distributing leaflets, and propagandizing the cause. He found that he was a fiery speaker, much in demand. All of this in the big industrial city of Tianjin.

In these days there was no time to think of a future career; the revolution was his life. But in 1949 the revolution triumphed; Mao proclaimed the People's Republic. Liu Binyan stood at a crossroads—should he go ahead devoting his life to the party, becoming a bureaucrat, a cadre, or should he embark on a more creative and diverse career? He had seen a bit of the world. He had been to Moscow a couple of times and to Budapest and Warsaw for Youth meetings. He had seen, as he thought, something of the West. To a young Chinese saturated in party discipline and rote rhetoric, these were eye-opening events. He found that in Communist Russia there seemed to be far more freedom for a writer than in Communist China. And in eastern Europe there was a new world filled with customs and images that came as a culture shock—a freedom in art, in the theater, in the way people talked and dressed. The theater seemed to these prudish Chinese youngsters almost bawdy. Women displayed their legs and their figures. In the West there was a diversity that could not have been imagined in Beijing.

And there were other things in Liu Binyan's mind. He had been shocked at the conduct of the Soviet Red Army when it came into Manchuria in the last days of World War II. It engaged in rape, destruction, and looting, not unlike the

Japanese. How could Communists behave like this? In western Siberia a little old Russian lady sought him out and filled his ear with tales of Stalin's atrocities—the savage repression and murder of the great leaders of the Red Army in 1938. He could hardly listen to what she was saying, yet it stuck in his mind. A few years later in 1956 when he managed to read a copy of Nikita Khrushchev's "Secret Speech" in Moscow about Stalin's crimes, he realized that the little old lady had been telling the truth. She was telling him about Stalin's killing of Marshal Tukhachevsky and the Soviet high command on the eve of the Nazi attack on Russia.

These impressions were too vivid to be absorbed at once. Liu Binyan had joined the Chinese Communist party in 1944 at Xibaipo, the dreary little Chinese village not too far from Beijing where Mao four years later set up his headquarters as he prepared to descend on Beijing for the final assault. Liu Binyan considered himself totally dedicated to the Communist cause. But in later years it would become clear that this truth-seeking man could not but be affected by these dramatic hints that communism and Communists were not the virginal vessels of man's idealism he believed them to be.

Liu Binyan was stunned by the dichotomy between the philosophy that he believed should lead to the perfectibility of man and rid society of evil, and the reality of bribery, power manipulation, pursuit of personal gain, and oppression of defenseless people.

The bitter portrait of Communist life that Liu painted led Mao to pronounce anathema upon him. Liu Binyan could not believe his ears when he was denounced as an enemy of the people. There must be a mistake. He sought out comrades who had been lifelong friends. They turned away. The powerful engine of Mao's apparatus crushed him. He was labeled a "rightist," deprived of Communist party membership, put on trial, and sent to one prison, one concentration camp, one penal colony after another, winding up in the wilderness where most prisoners perished of cold, hunger, and disease.

Liu Binyan had formed a friendship with a Soviet writer, Valentin Ovechkin, a man who had had his troubles with Soviet Communist discipline. Ovechkin's attitude toward Soviet party bureaucracy was not dissimilar from that of Liu's toward the Chinese bureaucrats. Ovechkin, too, wrote realistic reportage, novels, and plays exposing party corruption. Like Liu Binyan, he had been expelled from the party, then later readmitted. Outraged at persecution of Liu Binyan, he wrote an angry letter to Zhou Enlai who, in turn, became angry at the Russian intervention in Chinese affairs. Liu Binyan was blamed for instigating the Soviet interference. Liu Binyan had written a letter to Mao protesting his treatment. This earned him more black marks.

Liu Binyan, bearing the label of an "extreme rightist," was sent with a truckload of "rightists" to Yangjiangdi village in the Taihang Mountains for "reform by forced labor." Liu was thirty-three years old. He had never done manual labor. For thirteen years he hauled water, terraced mountains, planted seed, harvested crops, ate the coarse sorghum and millet, no meat, no rice, no wheat. The diet grew worse as famine caused by Mao's Great Leap Forward spread. In Gaotang County, Shandong, Liu saw peasants dying, villages turned to heaps of dust and sand. No one worked. They had neither the strength nor inclination. Women no longer became pregnant. Liu's legs swelled. He could barely climb a small hill. He hardly had the strength to drag a "honey cart" through the streets. He lived on half-ripe tomatoes and rotten potatoes stolen from roadside gardens.

On and on it went. Liu was returned to Beijing and set to hauling a cart of nightsoil from the *China Youth* magazine offices to a farm outside Beijing. His wife, Zhu Hong, was forced to denounce him to keep her job. Their boy and girl were insulted by their classmates.

Even after Liu's associates had their "rightist" labels removed and were permitted to return to work, Liu stayed in purdah. Months later his "rightist" label was taken off, but he did not get back his party card, which meant he could not resume writing, but could perform only secondary editorial chores.

In June, 1967, with the Cultural Revolution in full fury, Liu was denounced more violently than ever. He was charged with being a "class enemy," put into custody, and sent to a "May Seventh Cadre School" in Henan Province to be "re-educated." Day after day, night after night, he was subjected to insult and imprecations. He lived in the "cowshed," a shanty too primitive for animals. This went on for six years.

Even Mao's death did not bring Liu genuine "rehabilitation." That came only on January 24, 1979, after Deng Xiaoping was firmly in the saddle with Hu Yaobang as his right-hand man.

Liu's tag of "extreme rightist" was finally removed, and he was given his old job on *China Youth*. He plunged right back into investigating miscarriages of justice within the party. He ran into trouble. Liu possessed an element of naïveté. He made a speech in Harbin on Mao's role in China's horrors. A new case was prepared against him. For the time being it got nowhere. Liu Binyan went ahead and investigated a terrible scandal in Binxian County, just thirty miles away. It had gotten a lot of publicity in 1978; those guilty were Communist party members. The ringleader was a woman named Wang Shouzin, now under arrest. But in the county she still was called with affection "Old Mrs. Wang" and treated with respect. Those who had testified against her were shunned. Something was wrong.

Liu Binyan went ahead. The result was *People or Monsters*,

a case study in the abuse of power by the Communist bureaucracy. The woman, Wang Shouzin, had built herself a "watertight" kingdom by persuading one official to give her favors with which she bribed another. It fit together like a child's tinkertoy, all of them living off illegal food, goods, and privileges diverted by a network of bureaucrats. The bureaucrats lived high. They possessed almost any woman they wanted. If a poor family needed food, they had to put the pretty youngest girl at the disposal of some petty Communist czar. Women advanced in the party through calculated use of their bodies. Male chiefs waxed wealthy by charging underlings for favors. It was a beehive of corruption. Only here and there a man or woman of honesty stood out—usually paying dearly for his or her morals.

And—and this was the terrible part—the scandal of Wang Shouxin and Binxian County was repeated to infinity in the two thousand counties of China. It was a story of such universality that every reader said: "There. This is what is happening in my town, in my village, in my county." No reader had to ask if Liu Binyan had got his facts straight. They knew.

No wonder Liu's reader was overcome by a surge of emotion and smashed the glass he was holding. For each man or woman in China, Liu's story was *their* story.

And no wonder the bureaucrats targeted Liu. "We'll have his head," one in Shaanxi said. He was not joking. Liu's friends told him to watch for his personal safety. Liu did not take their advice. He went forward with one soul-searing exposé after another, one province after another. He exposed the corruption of a band of doctors, nurses, and party people in Xian. In Shandong he exposed a party gang that had continued without change since the Cultural Revolution.

Rumor after rumor was put about that Liu was being investigated anew, that he was spreading antiparty propaganda, that he was a sexual profligate. Liu was not deterred. He went into Liaoning Province to write about one of the most terrible atrocities of the Cultural Revolution—the execution of an innocent young woman named Zhang Zhixin, sentenced to death on false charges. To prevent her from calling out the truth, the authorities cut her throat so she could not scream. But Liu was diverted. He found that layer after layer of supporters of the Gang of Four still held their places in Liaoning despite a purge of top party officials.

Courageously, Liu moved forward. He had his party membership once again, and his party belief was strengthened by the support he received from the citizens of the country.

Political lines sharpened. A conservative-reactionary group emerged at the top of the party. The pendulum of Chinese politics was again swinging. Liu began to realize that there was no real follow-through on his exposés. Party inquiries would be made, then the waters would settle and nothing important changed.

Liu Binyan was writing for the *People's Daily* now, the largest circulation paper in the country, the organ of the Communist party. Its editor supported him. But Liu sensed that colder winds were blowing. He was right. Deng had begun to drop some of his best liberals. Hu Yaobang became more outwardly conservative, and his ability to protect Liu wasted away. The editors of *People's Daily* were fired. So were key liberals in the party's propaganda department. Liu published one more great exposé, of reactionaries in the Shanghai educational system. Then in January, 1987, Hu Yaobang was fired as party secretary, and Liu Binyan again lost his party membership and his right to write. The expulsion was published January 24, 1987. The headline read: "Libel and slander"—the cool response by authority to unpleasant but true reports.

Deng Xiaoping played a role in the second banning of

China's finest journalist, but a close-in role was played by one of
the dregs of China's political system, a man named Deng Liqun,
ousted earlier by Deng, disgraced by the party, but never losing
support from the geriatric hacks who stood at the party's core.
Deng Liqun, a man of striking personal immorality, was the
engineer of the coup that brought down Liu Binyan.

Every means was taken to isolate Liu Binyan, to cut his
contacts with his Chinese colleagues, the Chinese public, and
the outside world. Telephone calls were not put through. Travel
was restricted. At any moment, it seemed, he would be arrested,
tried, and sentenced to another long term in prison.

Before this scenario could play itself out, another began.
Liu Binyan was not merely a Chinese journalist and a truth-
telling man. He was a world figure. Harvard University
offered him a Nieman fellowship. No Chinese official would
approve Liu Binyan's departure.

But a friend of Liu's was able to raise the question with
Party Secretary Zhao Ziyang. Zhao (not yet dismissed) pondered the question a few seconds, then said: "Why not?" Soon
Liu Binyan had his passport, collected a U.S. visa, and was
off to Cambridge. He was not happy about leaving China but
knowledgeable enough to understand that it would be a long
time before the political wheel would give him a chance to
once again "Seek Truth from Facts."

Liu Binyan's parents had more than once read the tangle
of lines on his palm and concluded "this boy has many trials
and tribulations in front of him." They were right.

Though he was forced to live in an alien land, Liu knew
and said that he was "Chinese to the marrow of my bones."
He did not want any great honors. He hoped that when he
died an epitaph could be erected saying: "Here lies a Chinese
who has done what he should do and said what he should
say." It was an epitaph not many in Liu's generation had
earned.

18

Zhou Enlai

WHEN I LEANED around the doorway of the inner sanctum of Spiridonovka house in Moscow one autumn evening in 1954, I was astonished to see China's foreign minister, Zhou Enlai, behaving like a mischievous schoolboy.

Gathered at Spiridonovka, the Foreign Office reception house, were the chiefs of the then Soviet government—Georgi Malenkov, Nikita Khrushchev, Marshal Bulganin, Vyacheslav Molotov, Lazar Kaganovich, Anastas Mikoyan—and diplomats of Sweden, Switzerland, and England, those nations with relations with China.

Zhou, a grin on his face, was making the rounds of his Soviet hosts, glass in hand, offering toasts to each in English, a language none of the Soviets understood. The only persons who did were the three diplomats—and myself.

Zhou's conduct drew some surly remarks from the Russians. "Why don't you speak Russian?" Mikoyan asked. "You speak it perfectly well."

173

"Why don't you speak Chinese?" Zhou retorted.

Mikoyan's eyebrows knitted. "Chinese is a very difficult language."

Zhou laughed. "Come around to our embassy in the morning, Mikoyan. We'll be glad to give you lessons."

Kaganovich, his mouth full as usual, uttered a Russian "mother" oath. Zhou took no notice. He continued his rounds, clinking glasses and speaking English.

At that point a burly security man barred my view of the proceedings.

There was no way at that time that I could interpret Zhou's performance. I knew that he was sticking his tongue out at the Russians—but why? It was years before I began to put it together. That evening Zhou was on his way back from the Indochina conference at Geneva, the famous one where John Foster Dulles refused to shake his hand. Geneva was the first breakthrough of the fledgling People's Republic to world diplomacy, and, or so Zhou thought, it had been a great success. China was cutting its umbilical cord to Russia, and Zhou was celebrating. (Later he had second thoughts about Geneva; he realized that, as he told me in 1972, the United States had tricked him; it was not a real settlement.)

I was not unaware that beneath a sugary surface Sino-Soviet relations were not so smooth. But little did I suspect what intrigue, plots, and double-dealing was going on between Stalin and Mao. Zhou's little gambol was a tiny clue. He was kicking up his heels against the day when China would no longer be Moscow's ward.

Ignorant as I was of what was going on, I quickly fell under Zhou's thrall like every correspondent I knew who had contact with him in wartime Chongqing and Yanan. In those days he spent half his time with foreign reporters and diplomats, putting a friendly gloss on the image of Chinese communism.

It was not until the Cultural Revolution of the 1960s that I began to ask myself questions about Zhou and what really went on behind the facade of his remarkably attractive personality, his black-beetle eyebrows, the easy laugh, the sophistication. What, for instance, was his true relationship with Mao Zedong and Jiang Qing, Mao's wife, and the fearsome crew that stirred the dangerous brew of the Red Guards, the Little Red Book, the "struggle sessions," the assault on the "Four Olds," the xenophobia, the burning down of the British Embassy? How did this fit in with the suave Zhou, the world's most talented diplomat, the man who never lost his poise, the man who later was to become Henry Kissinger's favorite diplomatic sparring mate?

I don't know the full answers today, but I know a lot. Zhou's sangfroid, his charm, his social ease had roots in his personal background. Like so many of the Communist leaders, he was neither peasant nor proletarian. He was the scion of what he called "a ruined Mandarin family," raised by an uncle because of his father's dwindling means.

Zhou had been educated at the American-sponsored Nankai school at Tianjin. He was handsome, polite, attentive, the epitome of Nankai's creed (still hanging on the wall there in 1987):

Face clean, hair cut, clothes neat, buttoned tight,
Posture straight, shoulders square, chest out, back straight.
Beware of arrogance, hot temper and idleness—
In all show amiability, composure and dignity.

That maxim regulated Zhou's conduct all his days. Nankai was a molding experience. Here he met his wife-to-be, Deng Yingchao. Both were active in the drama circle, Zhou taking (in the old Chinese convention) women's parts, Deng (in the new Chinese convention) men's parts. One of Zhou's best roles was Nora in *A Doll's House*.

These were arts that Zhou would cultivate his whole life, and they gave an edge to his diplomacy. As Harold Macmillan once said when asked what he thought of Ronald Reagan going into politics: "My boy, we're all actors on the world's stage, aren't we."

In the central enigma of Zhou Enlai, his relationship with Mao, his ability to play a role may have saved his life.

It took me a long time to realize that Zhou began his rise in Chinese communism as a rival, not a handmaiden, to Mao. Zhou had been the founder of the party in Europe, had spent much time in Russia, and when Stalin decided to place his Moscow-trained young Chinese in charge and dump Mao, Zhou supported Moscow. He quickly emerged as Mao's rival, a fact which Beijing plays down since it impinges on Zhou's status as the folk hero of his people.

Zhou's rivalry did not last long. It vanished in the early desperate months of the 1934 Long March in which the Chinese Communists were seeking to escape annihilation by Chiang Kaishek. They had plunged into the mountain wilderness of western Jiangxi, and disaster followed disaster. In January, 1935, Mao came back as leader at a meeting place called Zunyi, Zhou at his side. Zhou never left Mao until his death forty-one years later. Whatever course Mao took, Zhou backed him. Through the nightmare of the Cultural Revolution Zhou not once raised his voice against Mao even when he himself nearly lost his life at the hands of hundreds of thousands of Red Guards, Mao not lifting a finger to help.

How could Zhou have given Mao such doglike devotion? After I published the record (not one survivor of Mao and Zhou could explain it), many young Chinese decided I must have been shown a secret document in which Zhou pledged lifelong support to Mao, possibly because Mao had some blackmail power over him. But I have never been able to discover such a document. The full story still lies buried in secret party records.

There is another question about Zhou: Why didn't he seize power after the fall of Lin Biao in 1971 at a time when Mao was critically ill and Jiang Qing and the Gang of Four in disarray?

The surviving marshals and old party chiefs to a man agree that had Zhou attempted a coup in the critical stages of the Cultural Revolution, he would have been swept away by the forces Mao set in motion. Zhou, they conceded, opposed the insanity of Mao and his supporters but perceived his role as that of "savior of the country." He saw himself as the conservator who must keep China from plunging into anarchy and dissolution. He believed there was no way he or anyone could halt Mao at his high tide of frenzy. He did not lift a hand to help the rugged and brave old Marshal Peng Dehuai or Mao's designated successor Liu Shaoqi because he believed Mao was determined to destroy them and anyone who tried to rescue them. Mao feared Peng's bluff honesty and thought Liu Shaoqi had won the backing of the party faithful from him. His paranoia pictured Peng and Liu as deadly enemies. There were others whom Zhou failed to save. One was the great general He Long. Another was the writer Lao She. Later Zhou apologized for his failures to keep them from death. In contrast, all he had for the widow of Liu Shaoqi and her family were a few kind words. He tried bravely but unsuccessfully to save Marshal Chen Yi, his friend and foreign minister. Chen Yi died soon after torture by the Red Guards.

It is a mixed record, but most Chinese give Zhou credit for trying. The young are more critical. They are apt to cite the case of Sun Weishi, daughter of a martyred revolutionary friend of Zhou and his wife, a brilliant young woman whom Zhou and Deng Yingchao brought into their family and adopted. She studied in Moscow and became a Russian-language interpreter for Mao. She also acquired the enmity of Jiang Qing by overshadowing her in a play performed in Yanan in which both participated called *Bloodshed in Shanghai*. The Red Guards, instigated by Jiang Qing, demanded that Sun Weishi give them evidence against marshals Chen Yi and Zhu De. She refused. Her brother was then arrested as a "Russian spy" and died mysteriously. Then they insisted that Sun Weishi give them information on Zhou Enlai. Again she refused and was thrown into prison where she died after torture on October 14, 1969.

Why did Zhou fail to protect his beloved adopted daughter? The best answer is that her persecution was part of an overall plot by the Gang to topple Zhou. He realized he could not save Sun Weishi and had to let fate take its course, hoping that if he survived he could still save the country. Not everyone accepts this answer, but few doubt that Zhou would have saved Sun Weishi if he possibly could have. Another adopted child had better luck. He was Li Peng, who rose to become premier. He was a son of one of Zhou's martyred comrades, taken under Zhou's wing. Educated at Zhou's insistence in the Soviet Union as an engineer, Li Peng was not happy in Russia, but when he wanted to leave Zhou made him stay and finish school. After graduation the Russians, finding him talented, tried to keep him in Moscow. Finally Zhou telegraphed them that Li's mother was ill. The Russians let him go home to see her, and he never returned.

On the surface the fiery death of Lin Biao in a Mongolia plane crash, fleeing discovery of his plot to kill Mao, seemed to give Zhou another chance to take the helm. Mao was bedridden, and Jiang Qing was quiescent. Zhou took the occasion to get Mao's approval for the opening to the United States initiated by feelers from Kissinger and President Nixon but made no bid to take over. Knowledgeable Chinese believe

Zhou didn't have the forces to win. He had strong support in the government and army, but the party was still in the hands of the feeble Mao, his wife, and her servitors. A coup by Zhou probably would have failed or turned the country into civil war.

These speculations became moot in the spring of 1972 when doctors found Zhou suffering from cancer of the liver—the disease from which he died January 8, 1976.

To me, Zhou seemed the consummate courtier. He courted Mao for forty years, and he even won Jiang Qing's favor by treating her as a lady. She had not met many gentlemen in a life that had started in the murky Shanghai movie and cabaret world. Zhou's diplomacy served to keep him in office and strengthened his hand in state affairs for a long time.

In the end, of course, Jiang turned on Zhou. When Zhou learned that he was doomed by cancer, he persuaded Mao to bring back Deng Xiaoping from exile and let him assume the duties of running China. For a time Zhou and Deng, aided by a temporary animus of Mao for his wife's interference in state affairs, were able to move forward rapidly. But as Zhou grew more and more ill, Jiang Qing made a comeback. She set her sights on Zhou and Deng and got permission from Mao to open an attack on "Confucius" (Zhou) designed to drive him out. Had Zhou lived a bit longer, he would have been hounded from office or worse.

In the closing months of his life, harassed by illness, hospitalized with excruciating pain, Zhou performed his greatest service to his country. He met almost every day in the hospital with several generals, headed by Marshal Ye Jianying, determined to thwart Jiang Qing's bid to succeed Mao and take over China. Even as he suffered the agony of his thirteenth major operation, Zhou advised the military on tactics and strengthened their determination to install Deng Xiaoping as national leader.

Zhou's judgment was clear, though his body was wracked by disease. No one in China possessed Deng's pragmatism, initiative, and willingness to take chances for the good of the country. If Zhou had given no other gift to China than that of putting Deng on the track to power, it would have been enough.

For this great service Zhou was paid back by Mao with a small but devilish torture. In Zhou's last days Mao caused to be played on Zhou's radio a poem that he had revised into a sardonic jab at Zhou. The poem dealt with a roc, a symbol in China of a man of towering stature and vision, and a sparrow, a symbol of a man with no vision:

The roc flies 90,000 li at one stretch,
Frightening the sparrows in the bush . . .
Don't fart, or the heavens will be turned upside down.

Mao, of course, was the roc, Zhou the sparrow. At the same time, Mao's aides refused a deathbed request by Zhou to hear his favorite old Long March song for the last time.

Whatever the historical accountants proclaim in their summing up of Zhou's pluses and minuses, his deceits, his weaknesses, and his achievements, many in China—and I share their opinion—see Zhou as a "very parfait gentilhomme."

19

Sue and Lawrence Brooks

FIFTEEN YEARS AFTER the Civil War four young Boston men took a walking trip into the Adirondacks and pitched camp at a spot in Keane Valley nestled between the shoulders of a mountain called Giant.

This was the beginning of Putnam Camp, a cold-water, hardscrabble institution which I came to regard as the essence of Boston-ness.

I didn't meet Sue and Lawrence Brooks there, but I was introduced to Putnam Camp by the Brookses and by my wife, Charlotte, all of whom had been Putnam campers in their youth.

Charlotte and I, of course, were much younger. The Brookses were nearly ninety when we met. They had spent a fortnight at Putnam in 1905, among twenty young people invited by Lizzie Putnam, a Boston maiden lady. Annually Lizzie made her selection with the aid of a Harvard man or two and a couple of girls who had just "come out." Her principle was simple: only young people of "breeding and character as well as charm" were invited—no one "whom you would not be willing to have your son or daughter marry."

Nothing had changed much at the Putnam Camp I saw since Sue Hallowell and Lawrence Brooks first went—kerosene lamps, an ice-water swimming hole gouged in a mountain brook, two army blankets strung on a rope to divide it into men's and women's pools, sagging-spring cots, bare floors, oatmeal, flapjacks, coffee in granite pots and granite mugs, singsongs and ghost stories on the "Stoop." You could drive in by car now. In 1905 it had been a twenty-five-mile haul by buckboard.

But the mountains were the same. Marcy, highest in the Adirondacks at 5,344 feet, Giant under 5,000. But the spirit, I felt, had not been diluted. Campers still had muscles like steel. They often ran up three or four mountains one after the other, galloping down the last after twilight to gulp bounteous dinners of corn on the cob, pot roast, mashed potatoes, canned peas, pitchers of fresh milk, and cherry pie. There were, of course, chaperones.

When Charlotte and I went to Putnam with the Brookses in 1974, they were still climbing mountains, scrambling up Giant, each with two canes, faster and brisker than we could follow.

The physical picture is daunting. But to recount the days at Putnam Camp and their beloved climbs in the White Mountains, Presidential Peaks, Washington, Madison, Jefferson, and Adams, sometimes forty miles up and down in a day, and their summer sailing off Cape Cod on their boat, the *Quawk*, misses the point. This was just fun. They didn't take chances. They did it with professional skill and sheer delight. Not exercise. They felt sorry for people whose muscles were not so springy and dashed off for a few sets of tennis to limber up.

182

The physical side was important because it set a way of life, and, as Lawrence Brooks once said, it kept his brain going. It did that very well. Another ten years of vigor and uninhibited opinions lay ahead for Sue and Lawrence when we first met. These were long-lived people, lean, keen-eyed, jolting down the stony path at Pleasant Bay, canes in hand, for a 7:00 A.M. swim every morning and a row and a sail in the bay after porridge, toast, coddled eggs, jam, and coffee.

I met Lawrence Brooks through a newspaper clipping. I was starting the Op-Ed page of the *New York Times*, and I was trying to find an independent-minded New Englander to contribute salty essays. The clipping told me that Lawrence Brooks was retiring as presiding judge of the Malden District Court October 31, 1970, after forty-two years, twenty-two spent as presiding judge. He was eighty-nine, and he had written the governor: "Time has begun to take its toll. It is best for the court and for myself to retire before this toll becomes too obvious."

His photograph did not suggest the toll had been great. He possessed a flinty face, a hawk's nose, sharp blue eyes behind wire-rim glasses, head held high, erect as a ramrod. You could be certain he was a man who kept order in his courtroom and would spot any flubdubbery in a flash. He knew who he was and what he was up to. I judged he might be the man I was looking for, and I was right. His first Op-Ed piece was a call on J. Edgar Hoover to retire as director of the FBI. Hoover was overage, the judge said—seventy-one. Brooks didn't explain that he himself was eighty-nine.

There was, I quickly found, no pretense in Lawrence or Sue Brooks. They had no trouble in sorting out the questions of the day. That had been true all their lives. If morality had not been bred into them—(and I think it had been)—they were conditioned to it by the Boston families they came from, the society in which they existed. They *were* the "New

183

England work ethic," although I am certain they never used that term and would not have liked it. To know their life was to know what was right and what was wrong with America.

I was surprised to find that they were by no means pure Boston stock. The judge's father had been born in Acworth, New Hampshire, and his mother in Lowell, Massachusetts, where, as Sara Cleghorn once wrote, the golf course was so close the twelve-year-old girls at the looms could look out the mill windows and see the owners driving down the fairway.

Sue Hallowell was born in Medford on Mystic Street, where she and Lawrnce were to live to the end of their days. But in the precise definition she was not a proper Bostonian. Her father was a Philadelphia Quaker who settled in Boston after graduation from Harvard in 1861. His father had been a Philadelphia merchant and foe of slavery whose customers were mostly southerners. Morris Hallowell put up a sign stating that he would not "sell his principles with his goods." He paid for his courage with a boycott by his customers that caused his business to fail.

The Hallowell rule of refusing to break a principle to earn a dollar was unquestioned in the world into which Lawrence and Sue were born. They would no more have mortgaged a principle than they would have sold a child.

The bond of the Brooks and the Hallowells was formed in the years leading up to the Civil War. The Hallowell house in Philadelphia was a station on the underground railway by which slaves were smuggled to Canada and freedom. Sue's older brother, Richard, helped organize and operate a station in Medford. They had family ties to the Boston abolitionist William Lloyd Garrison.

Public service, duty to country, belief in the fraternity of man—and a strong skepticism and insistence on matching facts to reality—characterized Lawrence and Sue, their families, and their Boston.

Sue's father was elected orator of the Harvard Class of 1861, but the college would not permit him to deliver the strong antislavery address he had written. He felt he could not let his class down by refusing to speak and depriving it of a voice. He elected to deliver the censored speech. Then he destroyed the text so that no record would remain of its milk-and-water language.

Quaker as he was, he volunteered and was commissioned first lieutenant in the twentieth Massachusetts.

Sue was Quaker born, Quaker bred. Never a cloud passed over her beliefs. Lawrence was a Unitarian and free thinking. His father had been a Unitarian minister but gave up the cloth to concentrate on sociological research and study of labor unions. He became a popular lecturer, a strong liberal, and, some said, a radical.

By the time I met Lawrence and Sue, they had spent a lifetime in good causes. Lawrence Brooks stayed with the Republican party to the end, but it was often a lonely place. The first and last president whom he supported with enthusiasm was Teddy Roosevelt. He considered TR "the George McGovern" of his day. He much preferred TR to FDR ("that tricky man"). But he thought TR's vanity caused him to fall short of greatness. He had no use for Warren G. Harding, whose administration he considered the most corrupt the country had seen until Richard Nixon's. He did not live long enough into the Reagan years to get the stench of its greed into his nostrils.

All his life Lawrence found himself fighting for civil liberties and human rights, first on behalf of black men and women and then in World War I and the aftermath of the Palmer Red Raids against patrioteers trying to tear away the protection of the Bill of Rights from Americans by depriving them of free speech and free press. He was fond of quoting

Samuel Johnson's pronouncement that "patriotism is the last refuge of a scoundrel."

He was deeply troubled by the Sacco-Vanzetti case. He did not think the evidence was convincing. What bothered him most was a remark made by Presiding Judge Webster Thayer to a companion the next day on the golf links: "Did you see what I did to those Socialist bastards?" Judge Brooks did not think a man capable of such a remark could conduct a fair trial.

In the days building up to the McCarthy hysteria the judge found himself in what his wife, Sue, described as a "situation of devilish things." The Boston Hearst paper mounted a campaign to block his appointment as presiding judge of the Medford court on the grounds that he was a "pinko." It troubled the judge a lot at the time, but he won out and thirty years later his only response was to shrug his shoulders and suggest that since the First World War there had been a downward trend in public morality.

On our first visit to South Orleans we discussed public morality at some length. The Brooks still occupied the sun-bleached, wind-swept cottage on the cliff above Pleasant Bay, which Lawrence's parents had built in 1887, not changed by a pin, the same piazza wrapped around it—well, maybe not exactly the same because the hurricane of 1944 had torn the original off—the same stone-scrubbed look, the pine walls sprouting ceiling-to-floor with the blue and red ribbons of hundreds of victories in hundreds of Pleasant Bay sailboat races, the Chickering piano, circa 1860, solid and square, soon to be replaced by the birthday gift to the judge of a Japanese Yamaha on which he happily banged out passages from Beethoven's Seventh or a Shubert sonata and sometimes the songs from *South Pacific* or an early Hasty Pudding musical.

With remarkable literalness, the cottage was a page from the late nineteenth century, a faded gravure of the Brooks family as alive and active as it had been a hundred years into the past, trains of grandchildren and great-grandchildren, blond, sun-bronzed, hair bleached to straw, minds crackling with answers to word games, Lawrence and Sue rocking in chairs by the window looking over the cliff, Sue mending socks and sweaters, talking about the Washington scandals, the dangers stalking the world, and of American character.

Perhaps, the judge mused, "family values" lay at the root of many American problems. He did not use those words, but his long years on the bench had left him with a keen knowledge of the formation of character in the young. Juvenile delinquency was real, and it existed. But he felt it was bred in the society in which the young people lived, the broken homes, the families in which there was no real parent, the adults so raddled with poverty the children fended for themselves. Poverty, Judge Brooks said again and again, was the problem.

The judge did not believe children had been morally better when he was growing up, but he believed public morality had been better. Certainly sexual morality had become looser. Whether that was good or bad, he was not prepared to say. He knew one thing. It never occurred to him when he was growing up to think there was anything wrong with the world, and, I sensed, he still did not feel that the world of his youth was on the wrong track. Today it was different. Of course there were things wrong in the world. Sue agreed.

She believed it started with World War I and that there was a specific cause—the mass of young people killed in that terrible war. She was not just thinking of Americans, but, of course, she had friends who were killed. The young men volunteered. They got into the war before the country did. Many went to England and France. As a Quaker, she felt the wickedness of war. She spoke of the toll among the European

187

countries, the millions of young Englishmen who did not come back from Flanders and the Somme, the French who died at Verdun, the millions of young Germans. Lawrence joined in. He spent early years in Germany. His father was fascinated by Germany, center of social progress and culture, the fine academic life of the German universities—lost, all of it lost—and then the rise of Hitler and the second round of bloodshed and terror in World War II. And the Russians— who could imagine their losses? Of course, said Sue, of course, it has affected our lives. You cannot lose the best of a young generation and expect the world to sail serenely on.

There was another thing that both felt deeply. This was Boston, the hatred in Boston, the hatred of the Southies and the blacks, the hatred in the schools and in the streets, and the politicians playing to these hatreds.

It cut very deep. "It just makes me shudder," Sue said. "For a hundred years we fought the battle. I am glad my father and mother are not here to see Boston today."

She was speaking at a time when Boston's race problem had reached one of its peaks. It would fade a bit, come back a bit, fade again. But it would not go away. It broke Sue's heart. Today, twenty years later, I do not like to imagine what Sue and Lawrence would feel about Rodney King and South Central.

In 1630 John Winthrop had written: "Wee shall be as a Citty upon a Hill, the eies of all people are upon us, soe that if wee shall deal falsely with our god in this worke wee have undertaken and soe cause him to withdrawe his present help from us, wee shall be made a story and a byword through the world."

This, to the Brookses, was holy writ. Boston *was* the Citty upon a Hill. Yes, it was not perfection. It had suffered many ills, many setbacks. It had, they had no doubt, outraged a reasonable creator many times. But year by year they and the good citizens worked to perfect their city. To see outrage done their solemn pledge distressed them beyond measure.

The judge and Sue believed in practicing what they preached. When on March 9, 1965, a young Unitarian minister named James Reeb was beaten to death in the demonstrations for black voting rights in Selma, Alabama, the judge, acting moderator of the Unitarian-Universalist Association, and his fellow board members joined the protest at Selma. There was no struggle closer to her heart and Sue wholly sympathized with the judge, but felt she should not join in what she considered her husband's particular affair.

The Reverend Martin Luther King, Jr., was coordinating the Selma protest, and Lawrence's delegation had strict orders to wear hats, stuff them with newspaper to deaden the blows of police billies, to avoid conversation with local citizens, even the drivers of the buses who took them to Selma or the police.

It was run almost like a military maneuver with the judge and his fellow marchers given shelter in a black housing project under the eye of the police. A service was held at Browne's Baptist chapel, and the judge explained his presence. "I'm a judge and I hate injustice," he said. "I love my country and I hate the image this action in Selma is creating throughout the world."

Lawrence went on to say that Sue's father, 103 years earlier, had recruited a Negro regiment, served as its colonel, and suffered wounds at Antietam which he bore the rest of his life.

"I think my father-in-law wherever he may be in the great beyond, will be gratified to know his son-in-law is with you tonight in Selma."

Judge Brooks died September 12, 1981, at the age of 100; Sue on October 10, 1985, just shy of 102. There is no monument to them in Boston, nor is there one to Sue's father, Colonel Hallowell of the fifty-fifth Massachusetts regiment, the second to be formed of black volunteers. But in the public gardens, the statehouse, and its golden dome looming behind, stands a bronze bas-relief executed by Saint-Gaudens to Robert Gould Shaw and his fifty-fourth regiment, the first black regiment to be commissioned, February, 1863.

One cool autumn day I went across the public gardens to have a look at it. The troops in the relief are mounted, and someone had branded Shaw's horse with a heart drawn in blue crayon. Each of the troopers' canteens had been carefully marked with a star in white chalk and the saddle clothes outlined in blue, not a defacement, a thoughtful and touching enhancement.

I copied down the words inscribed there. I thought they would do for the Brookses. They were: Death for Noble Deeds Makes Dying Sweet.

20

Sister Huang Roushan

THE MACADAM HIGHWAY that leads south and slightly east from Nanning traverses a broad semitropical valley on its way to the border of Vietnam. The countryside is not unlike that of southern California in the early days—lush vegetation, green irrigated fields of grain, orchards, deserts, and mountains, all pleasantly arid on an early June day.

Nanning is the capital of Guangxi Province, across the Formosa Strait from Taiwan. The people are cousins or even closer, speak the same regional dialect, and Nanning streets are filled with brightly dressed young women in high red heels and miniskirts and men in gaudy print sports shirts and suntan shorts. The crowds could be strolling in Hong Kong or Taipei. No suggestion of the stern and drab puritanism of north China.

The highway to Vietnam bustles this morning with private contractors hauling loads of produce on trucks they have bought from the army, shipments of fruit, vegetables,

191

early grain crops, flour, coal, lime, and other burdens snugly lashed down under black plastic. Only a few water buffalo and an occasional "yellow cow" hauling a no-springs wagon, but plenty of single-cylinder walking tractors carrying passengers and heavy boxes and bags on platform trailers.

For a bit more than an hour our route follows the luxuriant valley, but gradually the brighter colors begin to fade and turn desert-gaunt. Finally at a crossroads town called Liugiao we turn left onto a rocky trail that plunges into a narrow and abrupt valley, too stony for terrace farming and seemingly uninhabited. We have passed from a land of plenty into a wilderness—no cropped fields, no peasants plodding behind patient gray buffalo, no thatched huts, no moving animals or toiling people. We have come to a strange world in teeming China, a world devoid of life, barren, the air silent, no sound of chatter, not at all Chinese.

After twenty minutes of cautious driving around hairpin turns, along sheer vertical drops on a path wide enough only for a single car, we see a solitary dam cutting across a mountain stream, damming the flow in a crystal pool along the cliff and a wooden irrigation channel bringing the water to the valley floor. Now we swing around a hewn-out cliff and find ourselves confronted by a bulky fortress, strong-buttressed with heavy-barred windows, jutting from the cliff, grim and forbidding. We jolt around the fortress wing into a courtyard where chickens squawk and drying laundry waves from windows of two shabby wings, decaying across from each other. We have arrived at the Ching Ling Hospital, or, to give it its formal name, the Guangxi Research Institute of Dermatology, one of the sixty leprosariums still functioning in Guangxi Province in 1988. It was here I was to meet Sister Huang Roushan.

There were only seventy-three patients under treatment at Ching Ling, and by the mid-1990s it would, like every leprosarium in China, be closing down, its patients cured (or dead) and leprosy except for the vagrant case or two (mostly brought in from abroad) wiped clean from China's soil where it had flourished for millenia. Half a million victims were dying of the disease when the People's Republic was established in 1949. Leprosy had first been described in China in the great compendium of disease, *Hei Jing*, published 403 years before the birth of Christ. It was called an incurable plague and given the name Da Feng.

I had made my pilgrimage to this remote spot at the suggestion of an American physician, George Hatem. Hatem in the mid-1930s had cast his lot with Mao Zedong and his Red Army, had taken the Chinese name Ma Haide, had assumed Chinese citizenship, and for many years had devoted extraordinary efforts against leprosy. He had hoped the disease would be wiped out by 1997 so he could announce its extermination at the World Leprosy Congress scheduled for that year. But Hatem died October 3, 1988, and missed his great moment. It was likely that a handful of cases would persist after 1997, but long before that date most of the leprosariums, including Ching Ling, would have closed except as dormitories for cured victims. The thousands of dedicated workers in the leprosariums like Sister Huang Roushan would be transferred to other work or left idle, having given their lives to easing the plight of victims regarded in China as so vile, vicious, and dangerous they were hunted down like mad dogs and clubbed to death beyond the village walls when the telltale symptoms were detected. To be a leper in China meant certain death, either quickly and violently at the hands of neighbors, family, and friends or from the remorseless advance of a disease for which there was no known cure.

Sister Huang's life had been bonded to that of the lepers for half a century when I met her at Ching Ling in 1988. She looked out on the world with eyes of such clarity that, I thought, the purity of her soul glowed through them. She did not think there had been anything unusual for a Chinese woman to be a Catholic nun in a Communist country, dedicating herself in these remote mountains where no foreigner had ventured for years to the lepers of Ching Ling. I formed a different opinion.

Something about the inevitability of leprosy arouses a special dedication in those who care for the victims. When Sister Huang joined Ching Ling, there was no cure. All one could do was care for and comfort the victims, somehow to ease them through the inevitable turning of their bodies into desiccated flesh, the slow calvary that led only to the grave. I was later to see the victims whose disease had been halted by the new drugs, had looked at the wreck of their bodies and sensed the decay of their spirit, their heads hanging down, no glimmer of light in their eyes. Not everyone could endure these sights and go on giving the patients sympathy and kindness, not in the days Sister Huang began her service. There was no hope for them on earth. Yet, I thought, had I been a leper I could not have imagined a better companion than Sister Huang on that lonely walk to the end.

The early help for China's lepers was given by religious orders, Catholic for the most part. Without a firm belief in Heaven and God's will, it was difficult to sustain the strength needed to confront this death-in-life.

Because of traditional Chinese fear and hatred of Da Feng, there were no noble Chinese endeavors to ease the plight of its victims. Possibly Chinese pragmatism had something to do with this. Had there been even a whisper of hope for a cure, the Chinese attitudes might have been different.

Today, with the emergence of an almost certain cure for leprosy (unless the disease is not detected until its last stages), it is not so easy to understand the philosophy of those stricken by leprosy and those who cared for them in the days when Sister Huang began her life of service.

With the founding of the People's Republic, some of these early attitudes began to change. But even so, leprosy was far from the first plague to be attacked by the new Communist regime, and the delay might well have been greater had it not been for the energy and imagination of the American, George Hatem, who had been born in Buffalo, New York, of parents emigrating from Lebanon. It was Hatem who targeted leprosy and insisted on pushing the program. His influence with Mao Zedong gave it momentum.

Of course Sister Huang's efforts had begun much earlier. Foreign work with lepers in Guangxi went back to the last century, when Guangxi was even more remote than it is today. It had long been known as a great reservoir of Da Feng. As early as the 1890s a leprosarium had been set up by the nuns of St. Joseph's at Nanning. It survives today as the Nanning Skin Hospital, a leading research institution for leprosy. The research tradition had deep roots in Nanning. The region is a center for Shamyen trees, from whose bark Chanmungra oil, the traditional medicine for leprosy, was extracted. It is now known that the oil is valueless as a cure, but for generations faith in Chanmungra oil gave hope to victims. In the process the stands of Shamyen trees around Nanning were wiped out.

WE CLIMBED a rickety staircase to the second floor of the courtyard building and entered a long room, all windows at one side, looking to the mountains, with a narrow table running most of its length. It reminded me of a refectory table in a rather impoverished monastery. A light breeze made the room comfortable as we sat down facing the windows and an assembly of, I supposed, the management of this remote facility. The table was covered with a pink oilcloth, and I noticed at once that the windows were protected by heavy iron bars. This reinforced the impression of a fortress or prison, and, as I came to understand, the building shared the characteristics of both. The bars, however, were not there specifically to keep the inmates from getting out, although they did provide such a barrier (and perhaps, thereby, reassured the Chinese countryside); their main purpose was to prevent unwelcome visitors, robbers, bandits, or mobs bent on murderous attack, from forcing their way inside.

At the table sat eight or ten people, about evenly divided between men and women, doctors or nurses, I supposed. The youngest person at the table, a woman in her thirties, proved to be the administrator of Ching Ling. Of those present, she seemed to know the least about the place and its history, having only recently taken over her duties.

Almost directly across from me sat a minute, shy woman, in black dress with a face in repose, gold-framed glasses, eyes turned down, silently listening to Director Wang's rather confused sketch of Ching Ling and its origins. I could not guess her age. She had the figure of a young woman, but whether she was forty or sixty I could not tell. I found it hard to take my gaze away from her, and I thought I detected a hardly visible flicker of amusement as the director floundered about in trying to answer my questions, but she spoke not a word. At a loss, the director finally turned to her for enlightenment on how Ching Ling had come into being.

Sister Huang raised her head, looked directly across to me, the demure expression of a novitiate still on her face, and began to speak a little haltingly but gathering confidence as she proceeded, talking simply and directly about the founding of Ching Ling. She knew the story because she had been there with "Le Père Maille," a French missionary who set it up. In a moment it popped out that she was a Chinese nun in an order working with "Le Père Maille." I write his name

196

thus because, through no fault of Sister Huang, this was as close as the Chinese interpreters could come to rendering his name. The interpreters were at great difficulty. They had never heard of a priest, a nun, a Catholic order, or that there were many different orders. Moreover Sister Huang spoke in an extremely difficult mountain dialect, and it took three interpreters translating from one tongue to another to render her remarks into English. It took the same three stages to put my questions to her. She had forgotten almost every word of French that she had known, and my high school French was in little better order.

In bits and pieces with inevitable lacunae, with many a lowering of eyes, and sometimes girlish giggles, she told her story. She had been born and raised in a Catholic community in Gui County, about 130 miles from Nanning, but only a few miles from Ching Ling. The whole area, as she explained, was under strong French and strong Catholic influence when she was growing up, located as it was adjacent to French Cochin China. Haiphong was closer than Nanning. The French and the Catholic church had been active for years. Her parents and grandparents and almost everyone in her village had been Catholic.

"I come from a Catholic family," she said with pride. "We have been Catholic for seven generations."

She had joined "Le Père Maille" when he came to set up his mission for the lepers, she and another Chinese Catholic nun from her village. She was then about twenty years old. They helped get the mission going in the early 1930s and began taking care of as many lepers as they could rescue from the villages. Probably they were helped in this by the other Catholic Chinese converts. They had certainly drawn on support from the Chinese Catholic community as well as from overseas.

They did not pretend to cure their leprosy patients (the

197

contemporary director of Ching Ling was contemptuous of
their talk of modern medical facilities, apparently not realiz-
ing that custodial care was all that could be given lepers until
the 1960s and 1970s). All they could do at Ching Ling was
try to give a little comfort, feed the lepers, and protect them
from slaughter by the population. They dressed their appall-
ing wounds and did their best to save their souls. It could have
been frightening to anyone but a woman like Sister Huang.
No one knew how leprosy was transmitted and what the
dangers were of living in constant contact with the disease.
This never entered the mind of Sister Huang. She lived the
lepers' life and walked among them with the same beatific
look on her countenance that was there when I saw her. Her
faith was her shield. If God willed her to live and care for the
lepers, that was her profession. If he willed otherwise, she
was his servant. Year after year went by, and she walked the
inevitable path with her patients. They died, and she went on
to care for those still alive.

It was difficult work, as anyone listening to her could
know, but not a word came from her lips of its difficulty or
the danger symbolized by the stone fortress. That had been
built before the Communists came in 1949, but she could not
remember the precise year. Probably under the reign of Le
Père Maille's successor, another French priest whose name
escaped her.

The number of lepers grew. So did the number of nuns.
At a peak there were eight, three Chinese and five French
Canadians. One died but not, I gathered, from leprosy. There
was no sign that she had given a moment's thought to any
consequences of her service. She was a woman of pride and
faith, that I could see from her clear countenance, the way
she raised her head and looked at me squarely as she told me
that she was a seventh-generation Catholic. It was a little as
though she were telling an ignorant schoolboy the answer to a

simple question in algebra. Her pride rose again when I asked in bewilderment where she could go to church in this desolate land. In my naïveté I thought that it was not easy to find a Catholic church in backwater Communist China. "Why, in my village, of course," she said, looking over the rim of her glasses with a little spark of amazement that I could be so silly. Quickly one of the nurses (probably a Catholic as well) intervened, "And we have a chapel here in Ching Ling."

Sister Huang laughed easily when she had difficulty in making the interpreters understand the nature of being a nun and what she did over the years at Ching Ling. She looked across to me, as though to say, they are just children. They don't understand about these things. But you and I do. I was not by any means certain that I did understand any better than the Chinese interpreters. What I did understand was that year after year through thick and thin, whatever the demands of the lepers, whatever the perils to her life from leprosy or from working as a Catholic nun in China, she had never lost her serenity or her faith that she was doing God's will and that God would protect her.

I came back to the question, How had it happened that she had spent her life, since the age of twenty, with the lepers? She smiled. To her, it did not seem to be a question. Her life had simply been ordained. Nuns had died, some had left, but, *of course*, she had gone on with her work. What else could she possibly have done?

The coming of the Communists had not, especially in the early years, affected Ching Ling or Sister Huang's work at all. It was some time before the People's Republic with so much on its agenda got around even to acknowledging the existence of Ching Ling, and it was not until the 1960s that the new regime made an effort to integrate it into the national health system. It was happy to let the staff go on. True, the father who was in charge had left China, and not long after that the five Canadian nuns went back to Hong Kong, Sister Huang recalled. But she and the Chinese nuns stayed on. In fact, she still had two Chinese nuns working with her. No one had interfered with their work or their religion.

I could not resist asking Sister Huang how she had survived the Cultural Revolution. It had turned China upside down. Tens of thousands had died. It seemed unlikely that even the Red Guards could have disturbed this saintly sister, but knowing what I knew about the Red Guards I could not be sure. So I asked the question, Had she had any trouble in the Cultural Revolution? She smiled. The instant she did I knew she had had trouble. I had seen that smile too many times. It meant that she had had trouble, but that she considered it nothing important, just a passing cloud.

She said with dignity: "I was struggled with. I was paraded around." I could hardly believe my ears.

I expressed my shock. I had not supposed the Red Guards would have penetrated to this isolated place. Fear of leprosy would have kept them away.

She explained. No, it was not the Red Guards. It was her fellow workers at Ching Ling. She smiled again, and I knew that nothing they had done or could do would remove that beatific look or make her bow her head. Only God could accomplish that. I didn't think there was more to say. They had only struggled with her during the evening, she said. In the day she went on looking after her lepers.

I asked her if I could take her picture. She nodded. I took it and pressed her hand and thanked her in my poor French. She looked up at me and said "*Merci*," a girlish look on her face. She was, I know, seventy-two. I had asked her. Now she joined two of her fellow workers and walked away down the long corridor. She had been working with the lepers since she was twenty—fifty-two years.

I asked the supervisor what would become of Sister

Huang when Ching Ling was closed down in two or three years. I knew that they had been negotiating with the local peasants about taking over their lands—they had 12,000 mou assigned to them by the government in 1964 (probably the original grant made when Ching Ling was founded by "Le Père Maille"). The peasants would farm the land and provide food and sustenance for cured lepers who went on living there (most lepers felt more comfortable living in the institution than going back to their villages). Superstitious villagers often attacked lepers released or cured. They did not think Da Feng could ever be cured.

The supervisor was surprised at my question. Of course Sister Huang would stay on with the lepers. That was her life. She was, actually, retired already. But that had made no difference. She would stay at Ching Ling for the rest of her days, devoting what strength and spirit she possessed to her vocation.

As she had walked away from me, down the long corridor beside the heavily barred windows, she had looked back smiling a pert smile with a little gesture, as though to say, well, really, you foreigner, can you really understand what I am about? I hoped I could. I knew nothing of the Roman Catholic procedures for beatification, but in my ignorance I felt certain that when I had met Sister Huang Roushan I had met a saint.

INDEX

203

United States
  China and, 162
  Russia and, 91
U.S. Department of Justice, 129–30
U.S. Interior Department, 49–50
"Universities" (China), 7–8
U-2 incident, 90–91

Veblen, Thorstein, 25
Viet Cong, 52
Vietnam War, 2, 19, 34, 36
  Bigart reporting on, 95, 97–98, 100
  Halberstam and, 46, 50–53
Voznesensky, Andrei, 54–55, 56–57, 58–59, 60–61, 89

Wang Feng, 26
Wang Guangmei, 74–75, 77, 78–80, 81, 82
  children of, 75, 76, 77, 78, 79–81, 82, 83
Wang Hairong, 119
Wang Luguang, 26, 27
Wang Shouzin, 169, 170
War correspondents
  Bigart, 95–102
  Halberstam, 50–53
Washington, Booker T., 108
Washington Post, 126
Watson, Thomas J., Jr., 86–87
West Point, Miss., 47–48
West Point Daily Times Leader, 47
West Virginia, 16–17
Wheaton College, 128, 130
Wicker, Tom, 125
Wilkins, Roger, 123–32
Wilkins, Roy, 127

Williams, Walter, 154, 155
Winter, Robert, 5–6
Winthrop, John, 188
Wise, Isaac M., 108–9
World War I, 185, 187–88
World War II, 166, 188
  Bigart reporting on, 95, 96, 97, 99–100
Writers, viii–ix
Writers' Union (Russia), 59, 61, 92

Xenophobia, 3, 161
Xu Jiadung, 3–5

Yanan, 9–10
Yanan University, 2, 6–12
  language center, 9, 10, 11
Yang Shangkun, 75, 80
Ye Jianying, 179
Yenching University, 5, 156
Yevtushenko, Yevgeny, 54–56, 57–58, 59–60, 61, 62, 93–94
York, Bob, 52
Yugoslavia, 64

Zhang Zhixin, 171
Zhao Ziyang, 172
Zhongnanhai, 75–76, 78
Zhou Enlai, viii, 2, 9, 77–78, 79, 81, 111, 157, 161, 168, 173–80
  death of, 164
  Soong Chingling and, 116, 117
Zhu De, 9, 78, 156, 157, 178
Zhu Hong, 168–69
Zionism, 110
Zola, Emile, 33, 88